You *Can* Make a Difference

YOU CAN MAKE A DIFFERENCE

The Heroic Potential Within Us All

Earl Babbie

ST. MARTIN'S PRESS
New York

Design by Barbara Richer

Library of Congress Cataloging in Publication Data
Babbie,Earl R.
    You can make a difference.
    1. Responsibility.   2. Conduct of life.
I. Title.
BJ1451.B29   1985   170'.44   84-22900
ISBN 0-312-89673-5

First Edition
10 9 8 7 6 5 4 3 2 1

R. BUCKMINSTER FULLER
"BUCKY"
(1895-1983)

■

Who taught us all to be
Not passengers
But members of the crew
On Spaceship Earth.

Contents

■

You *Can* Make a Difference

1. A FORK IN THE ROAD

A hero is no braver than an ordinary man, but he is brave five minutes longer.

—*Ralph Waldo Emerson*

Twenty years ago, it was common for books and articles about the current state of the nation to begin with references to Kitty Genovese, a young New York woman who was stabbed to death in an alley early one morning. What made the story so powerful was that thirty-eight of Kitty's neighbors witnessed the assault without taking any action, despite her continuing cries for help. When some neighbors came to their windows to see what was happening, the mugger retreated. When no one did anything, however, he came back and resumed his attack. Clearly, each of Kitty's neighbors had the power to save her life. None did. Like the World War II Germans who did nothing about the concentration camps, Kitty's neighbors would later say they "just didn't want to get involved."

In part, the Kitty Genovese story made headlines because it fit the general newspaper formula that bad news sells more papers than good news. More importantly, the story dramatized a tendency many felt was growing in the nation, maybe in the world. Sociologists and others spoke of alienation in the big city, the death of community, and the lack of compassion one for another.

For some, the story justified their long-standing grudge against city life—epitomized by New York. For most who heard the story, however, it touched a raw nerve. We were unable to turn our backs on it, anymore than the moth can turn away from the flame. Kitty Genovese's obscene death in a Manhattan alley forced us all to ask ourselves whether we would have behaved any better than Kitty's neighbors. Retelling the story twenty years later has the same effect. No amount of evidence or protesting to the contrary can completely erase the nagging doubt we feel.

While Kitty Genovese's story is a depressing one, it represents only one side of modern American life. Here's a very different kind of story, reflecting a different approach to modern life.

A Modern Hero

Army Captain Robert Saum was driving through Oakland, California, on his way to work early one morning in 1980 when a pickup truck in front of him flipped over several times and exploded. Pulling his car to the side of the road, Saum leaped out and ran toward the burning truck. For the next half-hour, he administered first aid to the victims while the fire department put out the blaze and highway patrol officers directed traffic around the accident.[1]

Perhaps the most telling aspect of this episode was Saum's personal reactions to it. In the beginning, he reports, he felt a great deal of apprehension. He hadn't administered first aid for years, and he kept looking for someone else to arrive and take charge. "Each time I saw someone in uniform, I remember thinking, 'This guy will take charge.' But I was amazed. It didn't happen. It wasn't like TV."

Soon, Saum had taken on personal responsibility for the victims. He began giving orders to others on the scene. When a fireman started to hose down one of the victims, Saum realized that the cold water could cause hypothermia. "I made the decision that I was in charge then and I didn't tolerate that. I yelled at him to cut it out."

Finally an ambulance arrived. This was what Saum had been looking forward to since the accident first occurred. By now, however, his perspective as to who was responsible had shifted. When two ambulance attendants began to lift one of the victims, Saum stepped in and made them stop.

"I had a girl with a fractured skull, multiple contusions and abrasions, and unknown orthopedic complications. I didn't know what bones had been broken. I just stopped them. They said, 'We're in charge; we'll take over now.' That's when the highway patrolman stepped in and said, 'No, *he's* in charge.' "

Later, Saum would recall his feelings near the end of the episode. "I remember thinking, 'They're mine until the ambulance takes them away, my responsibility.' It was the same intensity of feeling I have toward my wife and children when they're hurt. It was like the whole family of man became my family."

These two stories describe opposite poles of modern social life. On the one hand, Kitty Genovese's neighbors experienced no sense of responsibility for anything they believed lay outside their personal lives. If Genovese was being mugged, that was her problem. The second story began somewhat similarly, with Saum waiting for those "responsible" to arrive and take charge. Saum, however, went beyond those initial feelings and took charge of the situation himself—even to the point of being responsible for the mistakes of firefighters and ambulance attendants.

Two Roads Ahead

These stories also describe a fork in the road for all humanity. The choice we make will determine the quality of life you and I will experience throughout the remainder of our lives, and it will determine the quality of life we leave to our children and their children as well.

While it is not polite to put the choice in such blunt terms, I know that you already see the signposts all around you today. As Americans, we enjoy a standard of living unimagined by our ancestors. Ours is the technological age. We are surrounded by video games, color television, great films, and all our other "favorite things." Nor is our national well-being only materialistic. This is also the land of the free and the home of the brave. The measure of liberty and opportunity we enjoy was seldom even dreamed of throughout most of human history.

Yet the glory of being an American is not without blemish. The fabric of our material prosperity is tattered by inflation, unemployment, violence, pollution, and corruption. Freedom and dignity are not perfectly realized for any of us, nor are they evenly distributed among all our people. And beyond our shores, 13 to 18 million die of hunger each year; a billion go to bed hungry every night, while you and I go to bed with the ominous ticking of a thermonuclear alarm clock. Life today, even in America, is definitely a mixed bag. Elsewhere it is less than that.

Charles Dickens could have been writing of our age when he began *A Tale of Two Cities* with this memorable description:

> It was the best of times, it was the worst of times, it was the age of wisdom, it was the age of foolishness, it was the epoch of belief, it was the epoch of incredulity, it was the season of Light, it was the season of Darkness, it was the spring of hope, it was the winter of despair.

The fork in the road is real. The choice is awesome. While it may be comforting to think that others will choose the route ahead, the real choice lies in us, you and me. You and I stand at that fork in the road, and we will make the choice one way or another. Truly, you and I and other individuals like us are the ones who will make the choice between personal, national, and global greatness on the one hand, or disappointment and despair on the other.

While everything I've just said applies to all countries, this book focuses on *Americans* at the fork in the road. In part, I do this to make our examination more manageable. Also, our prominence among nations lends special weight to our choice and provides us with a special opportunity, as we'll see shortly.

The choice for greatness, by the way, is not nearly as burdensome as you may be imagining about now. This book is not a somber call for self-sacrifice or for self-righteous misery. If my comments about awesome choices stir feelings of burden or guilt in you, that's not my purpose. That such feelings may arise, however, is very much a part of what this book is about —as we'll see especially in chapter 9—but before we're done, you'll be able to laugh about having such feelings. The choice for greatness, though it may carry risks and even some suffering, is fundamentally a joyous undertaking. Consider Trevor Ferrell, for example.[2]

Trevor was an average eleven-year-old when he happened to see a television special on Philadelphia's homeless people. As he watched the shots of men and women huddled in alleys, under bridges, and the like, he simply knew he had to do something. But what could an eleven-year-old do? The only thing he could think of was to convince his parents to drive him from their well-to-do suburb into the heart of Philadelphia's downtown. As they were leaving the house, Trevor grabbed a pillow and a blanket.

Imagine what it must have been like to be Trevor's parents on that trip. There they were driving around downtown Philadelphia, looking for poor people! Finally, Trevor spotted a derelict camped on top of a subway grate. Trevor was to remember him for the fact that he was wearing white socks but no shoes. Getting out of the car, Trevor gave him the pillow and blanket. Amazed, the man looked into Trevor's eyes, smiled, and said "God bless you."

Now the die was cast. Trevor had created a mission for himself. Two nights later, he and his dad were on the streets again, this time bringing one of Trevor's mother's old coats. Then he was back with more old clothes and with hot food. When his own family had run out of old clothes, Trevor began canvassing the community.

Word of Trevor's mission in Philadelphia was covered on local television stations, and the flow of gifts became a flood. Nearby Fort Dix sent him one hundred surplus overcoats to distribute. Gifts of cash made it possible for him to improve the hot food he was distributing. Someone donated a VW van to expand the family's capability. When Trevor put out a plea for shelter for the street people, a church opened a thirty-room house to them.

Trevor has become a special person on the streets of Philadelphia. William Plummer and Andrea Fine describe a typical interaction:

> Within seconds, Chico has spotted the van. He is walking toward it, crying, "Where is my little buddy? Where's my little Trevor?" Soon the derelict is hugging and kissing the boy, and telling him all about his latest ills. Within minutes, Trevor has calmed him down and now is tending to his material as well as emotional needs, ladling him a bowl of stew, fitting him with a new blanket and used clothes.

A somewhat different problem concerned Marilyn Keat and some friends in State College, Pennsylvania: America's estimated six to seven million "latchkey children" who return to empty homes after school each day because all the adults in their households are working. Keat, working with colleagues in the local branch of the American Association of University Women, decided to do something about the problem.

PhoneFriend serves as an adult, after-school friend for some 4,500 elementary-school children in the State College area.[3] Keat explains:

We call ourselves a help line or a warm line rather than a hot line. . . . We do provide help if children call with crisis-type calls but we don't want the child to feel that you have to have a serious problem. Children can call if they feel lonely or scared or if they think they've heard a noise. One child called because he thought there was a snake in the living room. We want to convey the message, call us for any reason. If you want to talk to an adult, we're here.

Trevor Ferrell and Marilyn Keat both represent a choice for greatness at the fork in the road we face. And they're not alone. There is something in the air. Studs Terkel calls it a "feeling of oats."

At this moment, in scores of neighborhoods across the country, in big cities and small towns, along dirt roads, behind mountain "hollers," there are people speaking out. They are turning toward one another, asserting themselves as they have never done before. Their grievances may be local—an expressway ripping up a neighborhood, a strip mine ripping up the land, an inequitable tax—but they reflect a larger discontent. Those who were silent are no longer silent, no longer accept the word from on high. There is a flowing of life juices that has not been covered on the Six O'Clock News.[4]

The "feeling of oats" and "flowing of life juices" Terkel speaks of represent something of profound importance for our society and for the world. The stories of Trevor Ferrell and Marilyn Keat, like the earlier story of Robert Saum, should not be dismissed as merely "nice." I suggest that our future as a nation will depend on the kind of personal responsibility represented in their stories. Without it, American society is in for some rough sledding.

I know this may sound a little overly dramatic. Living as an American today, it is difficult to imagine that our national greatness will not last. Sure, we are facing some troubled economic times right now, but those are certainly temporary. We've faced wars and depressions in the past, but we've always survived as a nation, growing stronger in the process.

Short of a thermonuclear holocaust, who can imagine the United States as a failed nation, a footnote in history? If you have trouble imagining such a future, take a minute to learn from those before us who shared the certainty that national greatness lasts forever.

Footnote Empires in History

Five thousand years ago, the first major civilizations formed in the Mesopotamian plain bordered by the Tigris and Euphrates rivers. Here rural villages were first transformed into cities and written language first appeared. First the Sumerians and then the Babylonians reigned supreme on the planet. Samuel Noah Kramer describes the first human civilization this way:

> Here, some 5,000 years ago, a people known as the Sumerians developed the world's earliest true civilization from the roots extending far into the dimness of prehistory. It was Mesopotamia that saw the rise of man's first urban centers with their rich, complex and varied life, where political loyalty was no longer to the tribe or clan but to the community as a whole; where lofty ziggurats, or temple-towers, rose skyward, filling the citizen's heart with awe, wonder and pride; where art and technological ingenuity, industrial specialization and commercial enterprise found room to grow and expand.
>
> It was in these Sumerian cities of the late Fourth and early Third Millennia B.C. that ancient man accomplished some of his most impressive achievements in art and architecture, in social organization, in religious thought and practice and—with the invention of writing—in education and communication.[5]

Had you been an ancient Sumerian, you would have lived each day as a member of the world's supreme people. You would have enjoyed the most advanced culture and technology on the planet. Even as a common citizen, you would have found a personal reverberation in the lofty proclamation of your king:

> I am Assurbanipal, King of the Universe, King of Assyria, for whom Assur, King of the Gods, and Ishtar, Lady of Battle, have decreed a destiny of heroism. . . . From my childhood, the great gods who dwell in Heaven and on Earth have granted me their favor. Like real fathers they raised me, and instructed me in their exalted ways. They taught me to wage battle and combat, to give the signal for the skirmish and to draw up the line of battle. . . . They made my arms powerful against my foes, who from my youth to my manhood were at enmity with me.

Who could doubt that it would last? Hadn't the gods of heaven and earth chosen the Sumerians to bring civilization to all peoples? Yet all that remains of Sumerian greatness today are archeological traces unearthed from under tons of rock and sand. A thousand years of civilization disappeared from the earth. Had you lived in those final days, you might have been the poet who cried in anguish against the day

That "law and order" cease to exist . . .

That cities be destroyed, that houses be destroyed . . .

That [Sumer's] rivers flow with bitter water . . .

That the mother care not for her children . . .

That on the banks of the Tigris and Euphrates there grow sickly plants . . .

That no one tread the highways, that no one seek out the roads,

*That its well-founded cities and hamlets be counted as
ruins . . .*

So much for Sumerian greatness. It would be comforting to
regard the Sumerian fate as a peculiar twist of history. Unfortunately, they are the norm, not the exception, for great world
empires.

The successor to the ancient Mesopotamian supremacy was
the great Egyptian Empire. For thousands of years, Egypt was
the seat of civilization on the planet. Social structure, economy,
and religion developed to levels unknown in Mesopotamia or
elsewhere. The arts flourished, especially in the areas of sculp-
ture and lapidary work. Writing evolved into a fine art, insuring
a lasting record of greatness. Giant pyramids offered additional
enduring evidence of Egypt's supremacy.

Unlike the Mesopotamian civilizations, Egypt has endured as
a nation. But the ancient Egyptians' descendants have a very
different place in the world. Today, Egypt is a Third World
country, a land of crushing poverty. Egyptian cities are greatly
overpopulated and chaotic. Disease is rampant. The nation's
economy is depressed and uncertain. As one readily available
indicator of the quality of life, the per capita share of modern
Egypt's gross national product (GNP) is $580 per year, about
one-fifth the world's average. As another indicator, one child
in ten dies during its first year.

Africa has been the seat of many other great empires of the
past. The Mali Empire of West Africa flourished as a powerful
trading empire during the thirteenth to sixteenth centuries.
Their descendants today are desperately impoverished. The
1982 infant mortality rate in Mali was 154 (of every 1000
children born, 154 die during their first year). The per capita
GNP in modern Mali is $190. The Nok culture of Nigeria was
a powerful force in Western Africa from 500 B.C. to 200 A.D.
Today, however, Nigerians have an infant mortality rate of 135,
and the per capita GNP is $1,010. The Kingdom of Axum

controlled Red Sea trade in 250 B.C., but their descendants in modern Ethiopia are struggling for bare survival. The infant mortality rate is 147 and the per capita GNP a mere $190. The current status of these past African empires is summarized in the accompanying table.

ANCIENT AFRICAN EMPIRES

Empire	Modern Nation	Estimated 1982 Status	
		Infant Mortality Rate	Per capita GNP
Egyptian	Egypt	103	$580
Mali	Mali	154	$190
Nok	Nigeria	135	$1,010
Axum	Ethiopia	147	$190

There are, of course, many reasons for the decline of Africa's great empires of the past. Intertribal fighting took its toll, as did European colonialism. Yet the African record of footnoted empires is not unique to that region.

Two empires dominated ancient Asia: China and India. While most Americans probably have some idea that China was once an advanced and powerful civilization, few recognize the past glory of the Indus and Vedic civilizations of India, marked by great strides in religion, culture, commerce, and urban development. Today, India is regarded, rather, as the epitome of poverty. Modern India's infant mortality rate is 123, and the per capita GNP is $240. Nor is China the model of an advanced world power today. While the infant mortality rate has only recently been reduced to 45, the per capita GNP is only $290. At the very least, both India and China are mere shadows of their past glory.

In the New World, the Mayan, Incan, and Aztec civilizations are often compared to their Egyptian counterpart. Great cities at Tenochtitlán, Machu Picchu, Teotihuacán, and elsewhere were the seats of great cultural developments. Had you lived in any of these great early American civilizations, you would have been convinced that your national supremacy would last forever. The descendants of the ancient Mayans, Incans, and Aztecs, however, live in poverty today, as the following table shows.

ANCIENT AMERICAN EMPIRES

		Estimated 1982 Status	
Empire	Modern Nation	Infant Mortality Rate	Per capita GNP
Mayan	Honduras	88	$560
	Guatemala	70.2	$1,110
Incan	Peru	88	$930
Aztec	Mexico	56	$2,130

With the exception of Egypt and China, most Americans probably have little recognition of the great empires I've been describing. (That by itself says a lot about the uncertain persistence of national greatness on this planet.) But let's look briefly at the empires most familiar to students of Western history: Greek, Roman, British, and American. Where do they stand today?

The world dominance of Greece and Rome are kept alive in history books alone. No one today regards either nation as a predominant world leader. While they have not fallen into the poverty suffered by the more ancient empires such as Egypt, India, and Nigeria, both nations face severe economic and political problems. By the same token, the sun has surely set on the British Empire, and the economic problems that trouble Americans today are worse in England. Yet early in this century, few seriously doubted that Britannia would always rule the waves.

The data on Western empires tell an interesting story. The older the empire, the higher the infant mortality rate and the lower the per capita GNP. On their face, these data seem to describe a steady decline of past empires.

WESTERN EMPIRES

		Estimated 1982 Status	
Empire	Modern Nation	Infant Mortality Rate	Per capita GNP
Greek	Greece	18.7	$4,520
Roman	Italy	14.3	$6,480
British	United Kingdom	11.8	$7,920
American	United States	11.8	$11,360

Explanations for the decline of once-great empires are numerous. German historian and philosopher Oswald Spengler contended that all civilizations pass through a natural life cycle of growth and decline. A similar view has been put forward and documented in the massive historical analyses of British historian and philosopher Arnold Toynbee. Marxist scholars, by contrast, see capitalist colonialism as causing the fall of many ancient empires, especially in Africa.

Demographic shifts are offered as the explanation for the demise of some empires. In a typical example, technological advances reduce a nation's death rate, and population then mushrooms to a size unsupportable by the nation's economy. All this is further complicated by high living.

The point of this historical sidetrack is to raise a question that should interest all Americans: What does the future hold for the United States? Will we, too, become a mere footnote in history: the Late Great United States of America? A casual review of world history strongly suggests the future may be none too bright.

The issue of American national greatness, however, needs to be placed in a larger context. The time when one nation could enjoy success at the expense of others is rapidly drawing to a close. In the years and decades to come, the quality of life we Americans enjoy will depend heavily on what happens in the rest of the world. If we seek to perpetuate a world system in which some nations prosper at the expense of others, then we will suffer the fate of great empires past. The alternative is to take responsibility for *global* survival and *global* prosperity.

As Americans at this point in history, we have an opportunity to transform the nature of international relations. We are in a position to bring about a shift from a condition of nation against nation to one of global consciousness and well-being.

Global concerns are nothing new to Americans. At the close of World War II, our nation took on a social challenge unprecedented in the history of the planet. Following the devastation of the war, friend and foe alike teetered on the brink of national disaster. Industries had been exhausted or destroyed. People were starving and dying in the streets. On June 5, 1947, Secretary of State George C. Marshall, addressing commencement exercises at Harvard University, outlined an American vision for the rebuilding of Europe. In four years of what was to be known popularly as the Marshall Plan, the United States provided 12 billion dollars of aid that was to restore the economic and agricultural stability of an entire continent. The Marshall Plan exemplified our national vision and commitment to the well-being of people far beyond our borders. As a symbol of this great human achievement, General Marshall was awarded the 1953 Nobel Prize for Peace.

Clearly, Americans are capable of taking on the challenge of creating a system of global consciousness and prosperity. And yet, it is equally clear that we are not now rising to the challenge. Indeed, we do not seem to make much headway in handling the internal problems that trouble us as a nation.

Year after year, we remain plagued by economic troubles, environmental pollution, crime in the streets. We make no substantial progress in reducing the threat of thermonuclear war. Politicians out of office condemn the failures of those in office and promise to solve all our problems, if elected. Once in office, however, they seem to do no better than those they replaced.

Every day, in many ways, individual Americans draw further inward, "looking out for number one" in a hopelessly "dog-eat-dog world." We grow increasingly doubtful that we can take care of ourselves, let alone care for others. Every day we find it necessary to give up a little more on our ideals, to be a little less the kind of person we want to be. Rather than make their criminal justice system work, people buy guns to protect their homes. Rather than demand an equitable system of taxation, people cheat on their tax returns.

Maybe Heroes Can Save Us

If we turn again to the historical record, we find countless examples of nations being saved from hard times and certain disaster by great heroes. When France was threatened by English conquest, Joan of Arc raised the armies of France to repel the invaders. Simón Bolívar brought independence to the nation that now bears his name. When Mexican peasants suffered under the oppression of dictator after dictator, Emiliano Zapata won them land and freedom. Except for George Washington, modern Americans might still be struggling with pounds and shillings. With Hitler's hordes poised at the English Channel, Winston Churchill stood up to save the day.

The point is this: throughout history, the threat of grave national disasters have sometimes been averted by the rise of heroes. Time and again, individuals of seemingly superhuman strength and courage have taken mighty stands on behalf of causes far larger than their own individuality.

Could America's current problems be resolved by a hero like those of the past? In our politics, we seem to hold out some hope for that form of salvation. We have a tendency to make our leaders bigger than life, to pray they can do what we cannot. In the end, however, we are usually disappointed.

I suggest that the root of our recent disappointments and the persistence of our national problems as well as the problems of our world lie in our search for the wrong kind of heroes. Science fiction writer and scientist Isaac Asimov looked in the right direction when he addressed the issue of violence on television:

> We've got to get rid of violence for the simple reason that it serves no purpose any more, but points us all in a useless direction. . . .
>
> The new enemies we have today—overpopulation, famine, pollution, scarcity—cannot be fought by violence. There is no way to crush those enemies, or slash them, or blast them, or vaporize them.[6]

The heroes who can save us today—both as a nation and as a planet—do not carry guns and swords. They are not necessarily taller or stronger than the average, nor is there anyone for them to kill. Most of their work will be heralded by little or no fanfare. You do not know their names, yet they will save us.

A clue to the nature of these new heroes can be found in the observations of Charles Ingrasci, a young American who went to India in 1977 to discover what it would take to end starvation in that beleaguered country. Most Indians, he found, were waiting for a new Gandhi. As he examined the nature of India's problems, however, Ingrasci became convinced that hunger would not end in India until the Indians could "find their own Gandhi in themselves."

Ingrasci's observation in India applies equally to Americans. As citizens of our nation and of the planet, we stand at a critical fork in the road. One road leads down the hill of continued national and global decline, to America becoming another footnote in the history of great empires and perpetuating the cycles of national rise and fall. The other road is marked by the creation of true national and global greatness, by the resolution of those problems that now plague us as a nation, and the opportunity to realize the vision of a world that works for everyone. We cannot take the turn toward true human greatness, however, without the appearance of a new breed of heroes.

This is a time for heroes, and we don't have time for anything less.

2. THE NATURE OF HEROES

Strong is the Soul, and wise, and beautiful: The seeds of godlike power are in us still: Gods are we, Bards, Saints, Heroes, if we will.
— *Matthew Arnold*

You and I are the heroes who will save America and the world. To prepare ourselves for that job, it is fitting that we take a moment to review, honor, and understand some of our predecessors in that job. In this chapter we are going to see what it takes to be a true hero.

There is one housekeeping chore that needs to be taken care of at the start of this examination. I would consider it a contribution to the English-speaking peoples if I could destroy the word *heroine* as the female form, presumably, of hero. I will at least do so for the purposes of this book.

In common usage, the term *heroine* connotes a helpless wimp of the female persuasion with her eyes closed or rolled upward, the back of one hand pressed against her troubled brow, weathering some unjust onslaught with a simpy kind of courage. She is very much the opposite of the classic hero; indeed she is typically waiting for her (male) hero to rescue her.

In this book, we are going to look at all kinds of heroes—*real* heroes—and they are no more likely to be male than female. I intend to call a hero a hero, not a heroine, heroess, or heroette.

Classic Heroes

I realize that when I use the word *hero* it probably brings a certain image to your mind. Though I will ask you to go beyond that imagery in this book, it provides a useful jumping-off point for our examination.

The Old English epic poem *Beowulf* describes the epitome of the classical hero. According to the legend, a great monster, Grendel, nightly terrorized the great hall of the Danish king, Hrothgar, devouring as many as thirty men in a night. The kingdom was at the mercy of the monster, until the appearance of the young Beowulf. Pledging to save the castle, Beowulf entered into a mighty battle with the monster, tearing off Grendel's arm and sending him packing to the moors, mortally wounded. When Grendel's mother, the water-demon, began terrorizing the castle to avenge her son, Beowulf again took up the challenge. Tracking her to the bottom of the sea, Beowulf killed Grendel's mother and returned victorious, bearing Grendel's severed head.

In recognition for his mighty contribution, Beowulf eventually succeeded to the kingship, where he reigned peacefully for fifty years. As an aging king, however, Beowulf saw his people ravaged by a fire-breathing dragon. Again, disaster waited in the wings, as the old man engaged a long and painful battle. His men deserted him, but Beowulf fought on. Eventually, Beowulf's sword broke, and the dragon sunk his poison teeth into the old king's neck, yet Beowulf fought on. In the end, the dragon was slain and the kingdom saved, but the mighty Beowulf had been mortally wounded and died.

Beowulf epitomizes the essential qualities of the classical hero: risking personal sacrifice on behalf of the common good. Yet Beowulf is scarcely alone in this regard. Achilles gave up his life on behalf of the Achaean attack on Troy. In the various legends of the quest for the Holy Grail, Perceval, Galahad, and Gawain provide models of sacrifice and loyalty. Robin Hood offers still another example of this classical version of heroism.

Theories of Heroism

Each of the heroes discussed above is a legendary character. While it is debatable whether they have any grounding in reality, it is generally agreed that the stories that have come down to us over time are at least partly fiction. Such heroic tales occupy an important place in the history of literature.

Prior to the appearance of legendary heroes, literature was focused on the godly domain: religious hymns and myths about the gods. Eventually, these were joined by the songs of wandering bards honoring human heroes. Finally, epic poems were written down, carrying from generation to generation the stories of mortal beings—capable of suffering and death—rising above the human condition to perform "heroic" feats. The epic heroes embodied the virtues of courage, sacrifice, altruism, and integrity. Clearly, they were intended to teach humans about their own potential and to inspire them to realize it. Thus, when Aristotle set about the task of educating Alexander the Great, he used the epic hero as his model. The young Alexander learned that he could be as heroic as Ajax or Achilles. In the process, Alexander was to become himself a model for later generations.

Heroes served a similar function in other cultures, though their form varied. Thus, Hindu heroes were typically great religious teachers. In Buddhism, they were most often ascetic renouncers of the material world. The original Christian heroes were martyrs. Viking heroes, by contrast, were more typically great warriors. Among the Onondaga tribe of the North American Indians, the legendary chief, Hiawatha, symbolized civilization and human progress. In each case, however, the function of epic heroes was educational.

In 1920, L. R. Farnell examined the manner in which the lessons embodied in the Greek heroes were perpetuated in the form of heroic cults.[1] He found cults arising around many different types of heroes. In addition to the epic heroes, some were more priestly in quality, some were genealogical heroes, others were demons. All together, Farnell identified seven types of Greek heroes who became immortalized through the formation of cults. In all cases, the heroes represented values that made life worth living.

In Farnell's view, the Greek heroes reflected the human aspiration to fully develop the quality of being human. The heroes showed the possibility of rising above the limitations of mortal life. In a similar analysis, Joseph Campbell has argued that the traditional heroes are a symbol of humanity's spiritual quest.[2]

Modern Classics

Though heroes appeared thousands of years ago, they are hardly limited to the past. Heroes abound in our own time. Many are clearly fictional. As a child, I grew up with Superman, Superwoman, Superboy, the Marvels (Captain, Mary, and Captain, Jr.), the Greens (Lantern and Hornet), Wonder Woman, and others I still remember, plus great legions I have forgotten. Not inappropriately, many of these childhood idols came to me courtesy of Hero comics. Others came over the radio airwaves: Tom Mix, Sky King, the Shadow, and others.

My son, Aaron, has grown up with many of these heroes, plus many I never knew as a child. I mean, Stowe, Vermont, where I grew up, was never saved by Godzilla or any of his kin. But Aaron grew up in Honolulu, and many of his earliest heroes came by way of KIKI, the local Japanese-language television station. In Honolulu (and presumably in Japan), this was the era of the Japanese superheroes. Some, like Godzilla, might be classified as benign monsters; Kikaida and friends were gigantic super-robots.

All these superheroes, mine and Aaron's, had one thing in common: nobody over four or five years of age believed they were real, even though many were portrayed that way. Who was the Shadow but Lamont Cranston using his "power to cloud men's minds." (Back then, it apparently wasn't necessary to cloud women's minds.) Captain Marvel was only a *"Shazam!"* away from little Billy Batson. Still, we were kind of sure they were just made up.

Some of my childhood heroes lived on the border between imagination and reality. Although I suspected that Gene Autry didn't *really* ride the range saving cowgirls and their mortgaged ranches, I nonetheless figured it couldn't be all made up.

John Wayne was surely the epitome of the modern hero while I was growing up. Especially when directed by John Ford, the Duke was unquestionably a "man's man." He was at his masculine best as a cowboy, a leatherneck on Iwo Jima, or as a fighting Seabee. While I don't suppose I believed that John Wayne actually did all the things he portrayed on the silver screen, I had no doubt that he was *like that.* I guess I would have been horrified to know he had been born Marion Morrison. Such was the stuff of those years.

One of the modern heroes of my youth had more substance. Audie Murphy, star of *The Red Badge of Courage* and other action films, was a genuine hero in real life: the most decorated American soldier of World War II.[3] During his three years of active duty in the Army, the freckled, baby-faced boy from Farmersville, Texas, was awarded fourteen medals, including the Distinguished Service Cross, the French Croix de Guerre, the French Legion of Honor, the Belgian Croix de Guerre, the Bronze Star, the Silver Star, and the Congressional Medal of Honor.

Murphy earned the nation's highest military award on January 26, 1945, in France. The nineteen-year-old second lieutenant was commanding Company B when it came under heavy tank and infantry attack. Ordering his men to retreat, Murphy stayed in a forward position, calling in artillery fire. When a nearby American tank destroyer was hit and began burning, Murphy leaped up on it and began firing the .50-caliber machine gun on the advancing German troops. Surrounded by the enemy on three sides, aware that the tank destroyer might explode at any time, Murphy single-handedly stopped the German advance for an hour, killing dozens of enemy soldiers in the process. Finally, wounded in the leg, his ammunition exhausted, Murphy abandoned the tank destroyer, and, refusing medical aid, led his company in a counterattack that ultimately forced the enemy to withdraw in defeat.

This was the stuff of which the traditional heroes were made. No wonder the U.S. Army chose to hold Murphy out to the nation as an example of all that was most worthy of our collective admiration and respect. It seemed perfectly natural that Murphy would go to Hollywood to become an actor. That was World War II, the last "good" war. Korea was to prove a national frustration, Vietnam a national crisis. Few Americans would recognize the name of Joe Hooper, our most decorated soldier in Vietnam. War heroes aren't what they used to be.

The Qualities of Heroism

What distinguishes heroes? In some eras, heroism has hinged on the ability and willingness to do great violence to others. This characterizes great warriors, juvenile gang leaders, and others. Great hunters do violence to animals: St. George and Beowulf, for example.

Even leaving aside those cultural traditions that revere religious leaders or great scholars, doing violence is not an essential quality in heroes in societies like our own, with its John Waynes and Audie Murphys. I suggest that Audie Murphy was not revered so much for the number of Germans he killed as for the *courage* it took for him to stand his ground in the face of almost certain death. It is clearly the quality of courage that lets us award the same Congressional Medal of Honor to Desmond Doss, a conscientious objector raised in the Seventh Day Adventist Church.[4] Refusing to kill, Doss served as a corpsman in the South Pacific. This excerpt from his Medal of Honor citation explains how a pacifist could be awarded the nation's highest military honor:

As our troops gained the summit, a heavy concentration of artillery, mortar, and machine-gun fire crashed into them, inflicting approximately seventy-five casualties and driving others back. Private Doss refused to seek cover and remained in the fire-swept area with the many stricken, carrying them one by one to the edge of the escarpment and there lowering them on a rope-supported litter down the face of a cliff to friendly hands.

On May 2, he exposed himself to heavy rifle and mortar fire in rescuing a wounded man 200 yards forward of the lines on the same escarpment; and two days later he treated four men who had been cut down while assaulting a strongly defended cave, advancing through a shower of grenades to within eight yards of enemy forces in a cave's mouth, where he dressed his comrades' wounds before making four separate trips under fire to evacuate them to safety.

On May 21, in a night attack on high ground near Shuri, he remained in exposed territory while the rest of his company took cover, fearlessly risking the chance that he would be mistaken for an infiltrating Japanese and giving aid to the injured until he was himself seriously wounded in the legs by the explosion of a grenade. Rather than call another aid man from cover, he cared for his own injuries and waited five hours before litter bearers reached him and started carrying him to cover.

The trio was caught in an enemy tank attack and Private Doss, seeing a more critically wounded man nearby, crawled off the litter and directed the bearers to give their first attention to the other man. Awaiting the litter bearers' return, he was again struck, this time suffering a compound fracture of one arm. With magnificent fortitude he bound a rifle stock to his shattered arm as a splint and then crawled 300 yards over rough terrain to the aid station.

Even though Doss refused to kill anyone, it would be difficult to deny his heroism, and his nation did not. President Truman presented Doss with the Congressional Medal of Honor on October 12, 1945.

Here's a more recent example of nonviolent heroism. The time is about four in the afternoon of January 13, 1982. The place: Washington's National Airport, blanketed in snow and ice. After several delays, Air Florida's Flight 90 had finally received clearance to take off and was roaring down the runway. Like his fellow passengers, Arland Williams, a forty-six-year-old senior examiner at the Federal Reserve Bank in Atlanta, was just getting settled in for the flight when something went wrong. After a dramatic shudder, the Boeing 737 smashed into the Fourteenth Street Bridge and fell into the icy Potomac.

Once the initial shock passed, onlookers could see a piece of the plane's broken-off tail section afloat in the river, with four people clinging to it. Then a fifth person bobbed up to the water's surface and was pulled to the tail section. Given the freezing conditions and their distance from shore, survival was uncertain at best.

At 4:20, a U.S. Park Police helicopter arrived on the scene. Hovering over the floating debris, they lowered a line to Bert Hamilton, one of the five. Hamilton grabbed the line with all his strength and was soon being lifted out of the water and whisked through the wintry air to safety on shore.

The helicopter returned and dropped its line to Arland Williams, who quickly passed it to Kelly Duncan, a flight attendant. Duncan was carried safely ashore. The helicopter returned and dropped the line once more to Williams. This time, he passed it to Joe Stiley, a severely injured passenger. By now, all the victims were suffering badly from the icy exposure, and it was vital to get them ashore as soon as possible. Stiley grabbed another passenger, Priscilla Tirado. A second line was dropped this time, and it was passed to Patricia Felch.

As the helicopter again lifted higher in the air, it became evident that too much had been attempted in one trip. Both Tirado and Felch fell back into the water during the transport. When the helicopter rushed back to rescue Tirado, she was too weak to take the line. At this point, an onlooker standing on the shore, Lenny Skutnik, leaped into the icy water and swam out to get her. The helicopter then proceeded to where Felch had fallen, and Rescue Officer Gene Windsor dropped into the water to attach a line to her.

Four lives had been saved. Now, thirty minutes after the crash, the helicopter returned to the floating tail section for Arland Williams, who had repeatedly passed the life-saving line to others. Williams was gone. His heroism had cost him his life. Gene Windsor wept as he described what Williams had done that day in the middle of a freezing river: "He could have gone on the first trip, but he put everyone else ahead of himself. Everyone."[5]

As powerfully moving as raw courage is, heroism involves something else, something common to the stories of Beowulf, Audie Murphy, Desmond Doss, Arland Williams, and Lenny Skutnik alike. Each acted out of a sense of responsibility for something bigger than himself. Each acted, in the words of the Congressional Medal of Honor citation, "above and beyond the call of duty."

Doss could have waited for the wounded. Murphy could have retreated with his troops, just as Beowulf could have passed by the court of Hrothgar as a bad place to be. Williams could have taken the rope for himself, and Skutnik certainly could have stayed safely on shore. Each could have gotten by with much less and not been criticized. Yet each took on a bigger measure of responsibility than absolutely necessary for their own survival.

This, I suggest, is the essential core of heroism. At the very least, it is the quality most needed in the heroes of the present and the future. What sets heroes aside from the rest of humanity is *the willingness to assume a personal responsibility for public problems.*

Defining Responsibility

I use the word *responsibility* with caution, because of all the extraneous meanings we've come to associate with it. Still, it is the appropriate word for my purpose, so let me define what I mean by *responsibility* in this book. Mostly I'll talk about what I *don't* mean. This will be a bit like the advice psychologist Jim Fadiman offers to those who might want to sculpt an elephant: "Get a piece of granite and chip away everything that doesn't look like an elephant."

H. L. A. Hart dramatizes the many meanings of the word *responsibility* in this marvelous paragraph:

As captain of the ship, X was responsible for the safety of his passengers and crew. But on this last voyage he got drunk every night and was responsible for the loss of the ship with all aboard. It was rumored that he was insane, but the doctors considered that he was responsible for his actions. Throughout the voyage he behaved quite irresponsibly, and various incidents in his career showed that he was not a responsible person. He always maintained that the exceptional winter storms were responsible for the loss of the ship, but in the legal proceeding brought against him he was found criminally responsible for the loss of life and property. He is still alive and he is morally responsible for the deaths of many women and children.[6]

When I use the term *responsibility* in this book, I mean specifically to *omit* any sense of blame, burden, or guilt. This specification, you'll note, rules out most of the meanings conveyed in Hart's paragraph.

As I will use the word, responsibility is *assumed,* not assigned, *undertaken* rather than imposed. I am interested in responsibility as a function of *declaration* rather than duty. This book is about people who take on responsibility where no one else would regard them as responsible.

By responsibility, I almost mean "ability to respond." We will be looking at people who come to life's circumstances as something they can respond to with impact rather than being the helpless victims of conditions beyond their control.

Let's shift to some mundane examples of living with responsibility. Imagine that you live alone in an apartment. You do not have a maid or a weekly cleaning person. Imagine further that you have invited some friends over for the evening, you serve them some beer and snacks, and the next morning you discover your living room has a number of empty beer cans and snack plates scattered around. Who would you hold "responsible" for picking up the beer cans and plates?

Before you too quickly dismiss this question as ridiculous, look at some of the possibilities available:

■ *You,* of course, come to mind and we'll get back to you in a moment.

■ You shouldn't dismiss your friends too hastily. After all, they probably created more of the mess than you did.

■ If you're renting the apartment, you might want to consider the possibility that your landlord is responsible for picking up the beer cans and plates.

■ Hey, don't forget the government. God knows, the mass of national, state, and local laws might contain something that says some government agency is supposed to clean your apartment.

The point of this hypothetical situation is that when you get up the next morning and survey the condition of your apartment, you are going to feel responsible for cleaning the place up. That is not to say that you will necessarily do anything about it, but you won't be holding out for someone else to do anything. Three weeks later, if the beer cans and plates are still there, you probably won't be blaming anyone else for the mess.

Now let's look at another hypothetical situation. Suppose you've invited the same friends over, but this is more of a class act. Instead of beer, you're preparing a special champagne punch you've copied out of *Cosmopolitan* magazine. Now, just as your first guests arrive, you realize that you don't have any glasses. You had planned to use those clear plastic lowball glasses you could buy at any liquor store or supermarket—but you didn't get any.

The point of all this is: How do you feel when you discover you don't have any glasses? Again, it's worth checking off the alternatives. You *could* inform your first guest, "No glassee, no drinkee," and help yourself to the punch. More esoterically, you could turn to your first guest and snap, "Well, are you going to stand there, or are you going to go out and get some glasses?" Or you could call a government agency. . . .

Unquestionably, you would feel responsible for getting glasses for your guests. You probably wouldn't even think about it. It would be that obvious. Even if you asked your first guest to run out and get some glasses for you, there would be no question about who was responsible for having glasses at the party.

Now let's consider another hypothetical situation. You are attending a community meeting at city hall. Someone has prepared a huge pot of coffee, but there are no cups. People are gathering around the coffee pot, making fun comments about the lack of cups. "It's a new program for people who are cutting down on coffee." "A cup! A cup! My kingdom for a cup!" "I knew I shouldn't have come here without my coffee cup."

Probably you stand there with the others, thinking up clever one-liners and waiting for something to happen. It's unlikely that you have the sinking feeling that arrived with the discovery that you'd forgotten the plastic glasses for your party. Clearly this isn't your responsibility; it's not your problem. Someone else is responsible for this one. You're in the clear.

There are people—you may be one—who would feel responsible in this situation. Not responsible in the sense of being to blame or guilty, but responsible in the sense of doing something about the situation. Such a person would probably start searching around City Hall for a kitchen and some styrofoam cups. As mundane as such behavior may seem, such people are the heroes of the modern world. They are the ones, incidentally, who organize the neighborhood to get a stop sign, who organize a protest against the threat of thermonuclear war. They don't necessarily look like the old heroes. They come in all sizes, colors, and shapes.

The New Heroes

Here's an example of the new form of hero who will determine the fate of our nation and of the world. Shannon Gordon was a patient at the Long Beach Memorial Hospital in California, being treated for aplastic anemia.[7] This disease, which primarily attacks teenagers and young adults, centers on the failure of bone marrow to produce sufficient blood cells. That dysfunction, in turn, lowers the victim's resistance to infection and is often fatal.

Aplastic anemia doesn't offer the most enjoyable lifestyle for anyone, and Shannon had every reason to feel sorry for herself and curry other people's pity. Shannon Gordon wasn't that type of person, however, as reporter Bonnie Ambler discovered when her own daughter checked into Long Beach Memorial with a blood disorder. Ambler and her daughter found Shannon functioning as "the self-appointed goodwill ambassador of the hospital's children's unit." Dragging along her own intravenous unit, Shannon wandered through the ward bringing encouragement and her own philosophy to the other patients.

"Gee, I'm just a kid, too, and I get needles all the time," she reassured Ambler's daughter, Heather. Shannon was a source of comfort and courage for both mother and daughter. Ambler reports, "When I was wondering if my daughter would respond to therapy, or even if she would live, it was Shannon who fed me the strength to face whatever happened. She was quiet and gentle with me in those dark hours, but when Heather did respond it was Shannon who led the celebration."

In addition to her regular rounds through the ward, Shannon

wrote articles for the hospital newsletter aimed at helping children and their parents to cope with serious illnesses. But that was not permanent enough, so Shannon persuaded the hospital's social worker to assist her in preparing a videotape, called "Shannon's View." The purpose of the videotape was to help health workers and parents to understand the feelings of children stricken with catastrophic illnesses.

What drove Shannon Gordon? Clearly no one expected her to take on a personal responsibility for the well-being of other children and their parents. And yet she was determined to do it.

As Ambler got to know Shannon, she found the young girl quite willing to discuss her own disease, as well as her fears of dying. As the reporter eventually discovered, "Shannon's greatest fear about the prospect of death was that it would come before she had lived long enough 'to make a difference' in her world." A greater concern than death itself was the possibility that her short life would make no contribution to others.

With Shannon's condition much worsened, Ambler spent one last night at her bedside. Despite her own pain, Shannon sensed the reporter's anxiety and insisted they talk. Shannon shared with her what she called "the bottom line": "Are you happy? Is your world OK?" Ambler concludes, "Shannon died the next morning in her mother's arms. Her life had lasted thirteen years—long enough to make a difference."

Heroism has no age limit. I stress that because we have constructed a formidable barrier to young people being responsible for the world around them. When they find discrepancies between our stated ideals and the way things are, they often speak out. And often they are put down for their concerns. "You are too young." "Things are more complicated than that." "You don't understand." "You're still young. Wait till you grow up." Such advice often initiates a lifetime of powerlessness and apathy. Fortunately, young people often ignore that advice.

It was largely America's youth who drew attention to the

persistence of racial segregation at midcentury. Young people such as Andrew Goodman, James Chaney, Michael Schwerner, and others gave their lives in turning national attention to outrage. It was largely America's youth who brought a halt to our national misadventure in Vietnam. And their contribution has not been limited to what some would regard as "trouble-making." The residents of Fort Wayne, Indiana, can attest.

Early in 1982, the Midwestern town of Fort Wayne was devastated by heavy rains and flooding. With the town's rivers threatening to overflow and destroy the community, it was Fort Wayne's teenagers who came to the rescue. Day and night they filled sandbags and built levees. As the waters rose, they built the banks higher. As the waters rose further, more teenagers arrived, and they raised the levees higher still. They refused to quit until the danger had been averted and the town saved.[8]

Jim Hickey, covering the story for ABC News, told of their heroism and dedication. "Those kids were already there working when we arrived with the cameras, and they were still working when we left. They weren't doing it for television. They were doing it for their town."

A similar quality was in evidence during the early hours of February 9, 1984, in Hayward, California. Shawn Ryan and his mother were asleep in their apartment. Shawn's father, a night watchman, was away at work.[9]

At around four A.M., Shawn was awakened by the smell of smoke. He leaped out of bed and made his way to his parents' bedroom, where he awoke his mother and instructed her to call 911 for assistance. While she called, Shawn soaked a towel in water and put it over his mouth as he led his mother outside to safety.

While the urge to save his mother might be attributed to some form of animal instinct, a broader sense of responsibility sent Shawn back into the burning apartment building and took him from apartment to apartment, banging on doors, and waking the other seventeen residents. Shawn Ryan was clearly operating above and beyond what we normally demand of seven-year-olds, and in so doing he demonstrated what very young people are capable of.

Often, opportunities for heroism arrive in the form of tragedy. At such moments we are offered the choice of retreating into personal sorrow or stepping forward to take responsibility for sparing others the same tragedy. Such was the choice facing Candy Lightner on May 3, 1980.[10] Here's how she describes it:

> On a beautiful spring afternoon in 1980, I drove home after a shopping trip and found my father and ex-husband waiting for me, their faces ashen and tears in their eyes.
>
> Steve, my ex-husband, said, "We've lost Cari."
>
> I patted him on the back and replied, "It's okay, we'll find her."
>
> "You don't understand," he said. "A man came along with a car, and killed her—and left her to die!"

As Lightner was to learn, her thirteen-year-old daughter had been walking to a church carnival with a friend "when a drunk swerved off the road and hit her with such a sickening force that she was hurled a hundred and twenty feet through the air." She was dead within an hour.

As if the pain of her loss were not enough, Lightner was horrified as she learned more about her daughter's killer. In the four years prior to killing Cari, he had earned three drunk driving convictions—and spent a total of forty-eight hours in jail! Moreover, at the time he killed Cari, he was out on bail from a hit-and-run drunk driving arrest two days earlier. Despite this unenviable record, Cari's killer was able to plea bargain "no contest" to a single charge of vehicular manslaughter and all other charges pending against him were dropped.

No one would have blamed Candy Lightner for retiring from life with her tragedy. Her friends surely would have whispered about how she should get out more, how she couldn't mourn forever. But they would have "understood."

Candy Lightner chose a different course of action: "I promised myself on the day of Cari's death that I would fight to make this needless homicide count for something positive in the years ahead." Forming Mothers Against Drunk Drivers (MADD), Lightner set out to reform the nation's laws on drunk driving.

In California, MADD was credited with prompting the nation's toughest anti-drunk-driving law, and drunk driving laws and arrests were reported to have decreased by twenty percent in the first month after the law went into effect. Moreover, some two hundred MADD chapters had been formed throughout most of the other states.

Candy Lightner is an example of the modern hero. Her heroism did not require her to kill anyone, nor even to risk her own life. What it did require was her willingness to take personal responsibility for a public problem she didn't cause. Where some heroes earn their stripes by putting their lives on the line for a few seconds or minutes, those like Lightner do so by committing themselves to the less dramatic day-in day-out work of creating a better world for everyone.

Heroism is still alive in modern America. And yet, it is stacked up against heavy odds, as we're going to see. Let's start looking at some of the obstacles that confront those who would take responsibility for public affairs.

3. THE RETREAT FROM RESPONSIBILITY

Self-trust is the essence of heroism.
—*Ralph Waldo Emerson*

Living in the latter half of the twentieth century, it can seem pretty difficult to exercise public responsibility and genuine heroism. Often our thoughts drift romantically to earlier, simpler times, when it seems to have been a lot easier to make a difference.

Whenever Gene Autry discovered evil-doing being done, he just threw his lariat around the bad guys and dragged them off to the old hoosegow. Today, Gene would have to apply for a roping permit, wait for seventeen government agencies to review the application, and ultimately discover that roping bad guys had been limited by legislation to the Bureau of Bad Guy Roping. No wonder Gene switched to baseball.

Organizational Complexity

A big part of the problem we seem to have in making a difference today relates to the complexity of modern society. Many scholars have commented on the significance of modern specialization, one of the hallmarks of a "developed" society.

While it's unlikely that any human society has avoided the division of labor altogether—organized around age and sex if nothing else—modern specialization is qualitatively as well as quantitatively different from that of the past. Here's an example.

In the years of the American frontier, few pioneers made their own wagon wheels as a matter of course. It was simply more convenient and efficient to buy them from specialists (called wheelwrights). And yet, out there on the trail through the badlands of the Dakotas, more than one pioneer built his or her own wheel under the pressure to survive. Under similar circumstances, however, not many of us would be up to hammering out a makeshift carburetor from an empty beer can. Or the next time your word-processor goes out of commission, you might try your luck at poking around the microcircuits with a paper clip.

Years ago, I saw a cartoon in which one person reported to another, "What a harrowing experience. The power went out on the escalator, and we were stranded for forty-five minutes." I remember laughing at the time, but now I'm not sure it's all that far-fetched. Every year, the technology that I love so much seems to make me that much more dependent on the expertise of others.

This mechanical phenomenon has a social parallel. Modern organizations are often so complicated as to be virtually impossible to deal with. No matter what your problem, the person in charge of *that* is likely to be in a meeting or at lunch, and no one else can handle it. You can be assured that the person you are complaining to didn't cause the problem and/or can't do anything about it. And these aren't necessarily bad people. You'd probably say the same things they're saying if you were in their shoes. The problem lies in the nature of the system itself.

Part of the difficulty lies in the sheer size of large organizations. In 1906, when San Francisco was devastated by a massive earthquake, the young manager of the city's modest Bank of

Italy, Amadeo P. Giannini, was able to get to the bank's vault and salvage about a million dollars in currency, notes, and gold. Shortly thereafter, he set up a tent and desk on a San Francisco pier and began making loans to finance the rebuilding of the city. By 1979, the renamed Bank of America employed some 76,000 employees in hundreds of branches to manage 85 billion dollars in deposits and nearly 60 billion dollars in loans.

Today's Bank of America, like any other large organization, can only function through extensive specialization, an intricate organizational structure, and firmly established bureaucratic procedures. While complex bureaucratic structures make it possible for banks to do things that would have been unthinkable in Giannini's tent on the pier, this represents a double-edged sword.

Timothy and Michael Mescon describe an experience at a bank (not identified as Bank of America) that is familiar to anyone living in a modern, specialized society.

It was December 15th, the middle of the holiday season. Overanxious shoppers were anxiously making last-minute purchases preparing to usher in the festivities. At the time, the man was stuck in line at the bank. His checkbook was at home, and in order to withdraw funds from the bank, it's necessary to have a withdrawal slip punched up. The line of customers needing withdrawal slips was long—very long. The lone bank clerk steadily responded to each of us requesting his services.

To his right sat another bank clerk, this one responsible for punching up deposit slips (not much depositing going on during the holiday season). In fact, there was no one in the deposit-slip line; not a single person. The deposit clerk sat there, completing a crossword puzzle, clipping his nails and eating a pastrami sandwich. In short, the deposit clerk wasn't very busy.

By the time the customer finally reached the withdrawal clerk, the slip was quickly processed. As he walked away, on a whim, the customer remarked to the deposit clerk, "Excuse me, you might want to consider helping out with some of these withdrawal slips. After all, it's not very complicated, and your co-worker is swamped." In response to this comment, the clerk looked up and responded, "I know how, but it's not my job."[1]

During the 1960s, the nation's large corporations, as well as the federal government, didn't fare too well on college and university campuses, being held generally responsible for the war in Vietnam, domestic poverty, racial discrimination, and the like. At the same time, a more sophisticated, radical critique held that the problems of American society were not so much the fault of the individual leaders as of "the system"—meaning the *capitalist* system. Thus, for example, the "military-industrial complex" had an ominous existence that far surpassed any particular military or industrial figures.

In retrospect, I think this was a useful breakthrough in our understanding of modern social life, but it was only a way station, not the final destination. The real problem, I suggest, lies not in *the* system but in *system,* per se. Capitalists have nothing on socialists in this respect. Both systems seem fully capable of botching things up. Something more fundamental is involved.

Structuring Responsibility

It is in the nature of complex social systems—of any political flavor—to destroy personal responsibility by structuring it. In our modern corporations and governmental agencies, we have created the illusion of responsibility. The goal was a laudable one, but the result has been less than ideal, as we'll see.

We have recognized that the average individuals in a modern society are unable to protect themselves from the failings of specialists. When you go to the supermarket, for example, and purchase a carton of milk, you really have no way of being sure the milk is pure. How can you tell if the new diet pills you purchased through an ad in a movie magazine are going to kill you? You have no way of knowing if the brakes are going to fail on your new car.

In view of the fact that each of us will be dependent on thousands and thousands of people whom we'll never see— dependent on them to do their jobs properly but unable to make sure they do—we have assigned the responsibility for such matters to other specialists. Thus, for example, the Food and Drug Administration has been assigned the responsibility of guaranteeing that the food and drugs offered for sale to us are pure. By specializing in that task, they can do a better job than either you or I could do on our own behalf.

Of course, the sheer size of our society precludes one specialist from taking on such a job. Thus the Food and Drug Administration employs thousands of subspecialists, each assigned a somewhat narrower range of responsibility. On the face of it, all this would seem to make sense—except for how it turns out.

As the assignment of responsibility itself gets more complex, it gets more ambiguous. Eventually, when something goes wrong, it isn't altogether clear which subspecialist dropped the ball. Often we find co-workers blaming each other, departments placing responsibility with other departments, and so forth.

All this gets worse yet when politics enters the picture—as it inevitably does. As soon as a government agency is created to monitor some branch of industry, individual companies and trade associations create lobbying arms to deal with the agency, and we hear charges that the lobbyists have tried to circumvent or even corrupt the agency.

Actually, the formal structuring of responsibility has a negative impact on us all. Not only are we less likely to *take* responsibility than before that responsibility was assigned to someone else; we become more *ir*responsible.

First, the system of structured responsibility we've created sets up automatic, personal responses that rob us of the experience of responsibility. We set a machine in motion that makes it "normal" to feel someone else is responsible for how things turn out. We give up responsibility for solving the problems we observe around us.

Then, to make matters worse, the system we've created encourages us to *create* problems. Once we've hired a lifeguard for the beach, you and I feel we can swim out as far as we want, because it's the lifeguard's responsibility to tell us if we're taking a chance and to save us if we get into trouble. Once we hire a police force, we feel free to wander into Harlem on a Saturday night and start calling folks "niggers." (Or, depending on your racial persuasion, you can drive through Biloxi and yell "Honky!" at the good ole boys.)

This phenomenon starts an intricate process that I'm sure is familiar to you. Let's look at an example of how it works. Consider the lowly beer can.

The Parable of the Beer Can

Let's suppose that we live in a small community that is littering one hundred beer cans a day on the grounds of the community park. That's a problem, and to solve the problem we hire one worker to have the responsibility of picking up the cans. We figure that one worker can walk around the park and pick up one hundred beer cans a day. Having created that arrangement, however, we can now let go of whatever self-restraint we have been exercising and toss the rest of our beer cans on the ground, creating a new total of two hundred cans a day.

Our one worker now cannot get the job done and demands that more help be hired. You and I are irritated, too, because we're paying to have the park kept clean and it's as messy as before. So, to get the problem handled once and for all, we hire another person to pick up cans, a third to patrol the park and arrest anyone caught littering, and a fourth to supervise the other three.

By now we are paying a goodly sum to have our park kept clean. It has now become our right as tax-paying American citizens to have a clean park—even if we do throw our cans on the ground. Having created a system working against our littering, however, we have created an adversary system: "us" versus "them." Of course, we could avoid the adversary system altogether by simply throwing our beer cans in the trash barrel, but if we did that, what would be the justification for paying all those taxes? Those lazy bastards on the park's crew would sit around all day drinking coffee, not lifting a finger to earn their piece of the taxes you and I are paying. Not wanting to get arrested, however, we toss the beer cans in the bushes so no one will see what we did. That tactic makes the trash harder to pick up and requires an increase in the park's crew. Now we need two teams of three workers each and a supervisor for each team, and the original supervisor is now elevated to parks director in a downtown office with a private secretary and a payroll clerk.

By now the park workers have decided that it's undignified to pick up other people's trash and have formed a union to demand more pay in compensation for the indignity of the work. The parks director now requires a collective-bargaining specialist who, in turn, needs his or her own office and secretary, plus an annual trip to the meetings of the Association of Municipal Collective-Bargaining Specialists at Miami Beach (with per diem). To combat the growing effectiveness of the collective-bargaining specialist in City Hall, the Park Workers Local 33 now needs to expand the union staff, requiring increased union dues, requiring increased pay for the workers so they can pay the increased dues. This outrageous increase in park-worker pay creates a flap at City Hall, and the collective-bargaining specialist is given two assistants, each of whom requires a secretary and trips to the regional meetings of the A.M.C.B.S. (in Kansas City). Now, the parks department payroll clerk needs an assistant, and the director needs an assistant director for personnel and an executive secretary. A municipal bond is floated to construct a new building to house the department. The building costs ten million dollars and is located on what was originally our park.

At last, we have eliminated the problem of beer cans in the park. We have also eliminated the park, but somehow the workers, the supervisors and staff, and the union still find things to do so as to justify our continued payment of taxes as well as the repayment of the bond on the new building. Maybe we should have just thrown the goddamn cans in the trash barrel in the first place.

I have always had the feeling that this little parable would be a lot funnier if it weren't so true. Each of us has seen comparable chains of events, and we usually didn't regard them as comedy. For many Americans, the current state of civilization is downright depressing.

Taking Responsibility in Government

The lack of personal responsibility within large organizations is nowhere more evident than within the government, especially the federal government. Stories of uncaring, unthinking, and irresponsible bureaucratic misbehavior are legion. There are, however, a great many exceptions, who stand as living proof that individuals can take personal responsibility even within government.

Listen to Harlan Cleveland, formerly the U.S. ambassador to NATO, recall the late senator and vice president, Hubert Humphrey:

> . . . Humphrey is a public service role model because he was literally interested in everything. He was blessed with an intellectual curiosity that embraced the world, spanned the oceans, and extended into outer space. As a "situation-as-a-whole" person, he felt a personal responsibility for growing more food, making useful goods, distributing wealth fairly, creating better jobs, combatting inflation, managing government, and ensuring international peace. Everything was his personal responsibility. We need about a million more people like him.

Cleveland is currently director of the Hubert H. Humphrey Institute of Public Affairs at the University of Minnesota. After a lifetime of public service, Cleveland takes any opportunity that presents itself to draw attention to excellence in government. Following World War II, Cleveland worked on the administration of the Marshall Plan. Here, he describes his boss, Paul Hoffman.

Perhaps because he had been a major executive and a major business leader before he came into the government to run the Marshall Plan, Paul Hoffman had a well-developed sense of personal confidence. More than that, he had a feeling that whatever was wrong in the organization of the U.S. government, or in Europe, it was always his turn to do something about it. It was never the moment for him to sit down and wait for somebody else to do something. He always felt that somehow he should be taking the initiative.[2]

Lucy Andris is a young social worker at a Chicago hospital. One wintry morning in 1981, one of the staff doctors called to ask her assistance. The patient in question was a man of sixty-nine, who had been brought to the hospital by his seventy-two-year-old wife. Both were ill, the husband with a severe heart problem.[3]

The doctors had found several prescriptions in the man's pocket, but he simply didn't have enough money to get them filled. Simple enough: Andris would get government assistance for him. But it wasn't that simple.

The regulations governing financial assistance set a monthly income limit of $333 for recipients. The couple whom Andris wanted to help was receiving disability and Social Security payments totalling $477 a month. They were simply too "wealthy" to receive assistance. The more Andris pursued the matter, the more frustrating she found the cobweb of regulations. For example, if the man could run up a total of $714 in unpaid medical expenses over a six-month period, then he would qualify for assistance. Not too practical for someone doctors said might die if he didn't get his medicine soon.

As Andris went to the couple's slum apartment to explain that nothing could be done, we can imagine some of what must have been running through her mind. "I didn't make the rules. In fact, I think they're stupid. I'll keep trying to find a loophole." Before she could say any of that, she recognized that she had made them her personal responsibility. She stopped at a drugstore and paid $47 of her own money to fill the prescriptions. She knew social workers weren't supposed to get "too involved" in their cases. Living on a tight budget herself, she recognized that she couldn't personally pay for all the needy. But all that paled in the knowledge that she had saved an old man's life.

In American folklore, the school truant officer represents the epitome of the "heavy" in adversarial relationships. The officer is on one side, the truants on the other, and the question is who can outsmart whom. James McSherry, supervisor of attendance in the Boston school system, raises havoc with that stereotype, however.[4]

McSherry makes relatively few arrests, for example, preferring to find other solutions. Moreover, he is especially sensitive to the real reasons for school absences. In one case, for example, he noticed that a student was always absent on the fifteenth and thirtieth of the month. Looking further into the matter, McSherry discovered that the student's mother had him stay by the mailbox all day to ensure that their welfare check wouldn't be stolen. McSherry chose to look the other way, feeling the need for the child at home was more compelling than having him in school.

Although his official job description would not require him to go beyond attendance matters in his dealings with students, McSherry goes out of his way to support students any way he can. Visiting one truant, he found a number of paintings on the wall. When he discovered the student had painted them, he set about getting the student in touch with art schools. Although pregnant students are not required to attend school, McSherry always encourages them to attend classes at alternative facilities so they can return to school after their children are born. Because of his obvious commitment to the well-being of all the students he deals with, this unusual truant officer can visit the roughest of Boston's neighborhoods without fear.

A special class of governmental heroes go by the name of *whistle-blower.* The best known, surely, is Ernest Fitzgerald, a civilian management specialist with the Air Force.[5] In 1968, he startled his employers by testifying before the Congress regarding cost overruns. In particular, he pointed out that the C-5A transport plane would cost $2 billion more than they planned.

As a reward for his courage, the Air Force fired Fitzgerald. He spent the next fourteen years in court, winning his job back. In retrospect, Fitzgerald told reporter Rebecca Nappi, "You never recover. Having gotten into it, I wasn't going to lie, but it was a personal disaster. It ruined my career." He's not thrilled with the term *whistle-blower,* feeling it implies someone who is a little strange. As Fitzgerald insists, "Telling the truth should become routine."

Fitzgerald's willingness to step forward and tell the truth has made it that much easier for other government employees to take similar actions. Perhaps eventually we shall see a realization of Fitzgerald's view about truth becoming routine.

For the time being, however, the overall experience of personal integrity and responsibility in government falls short of Fitzgerald's vision. That situation fits hand-in-glove with the general public's image of government and interactions with it.

Alienation and Disenchantment

In November 1981, the Roper Organization, a nationally respected polling firm, conducted a survey to measure what they called the "Gross National Spirit." In a number of respects, they found spirits dampened.

For example, the survey asked a national sample of adults: "In general, how satisfied are you with the way things are going in the United States today? Are you very satisfied, more or less satisfied, or not at all satisfied?" Here's what they answered:

Very satisfied 7%

More or less satisfied......................... 47%

Not at all satisfied 46%

Nor were the Americans surveyed especially hopeful for the future. When asked, "Over the next year, do you think things will go better for the United States, go worse, or stay about the same?" the largest percentage said they thought things would get worse:

Will get better 28%

Stay about the same.......................... 29%

Will get worse 43%

Although 69 percent of those interviewed said it is still possible "to start out poor and become rich by working hard," three-fourths said it was harder to get ahead financially than it was twenty-five years ago.[6]

By the same token, a 1982 survey by the National Opinion Research Center found 68 percent of American adults agreeing with the statement: "The lot of the average man is getting worse." This was an increase from the 56 percent who agreed in 1973.

Nowhere is modern American alienation more evident than in people's attitudes toward their government and who it serves. In 1958, for example, a national sample of Americans were asked whether they felt the government was run for "the benefit of all" or "a few big interests looking out for themselves." In the midst of the Eisenhower years, 82 percent said government was run for the benefit of all. When the same question was asked of a national sample in 1980, a mere 23 percent would say government was run for the benefit of all; over three-fourths felt it was run on behalf of a few big interests.

In the same surveys, people were asked whether they would "trust the government in Washington to do what is right." In 1958, 16 percent said "always" and another 59 percent said "most of the time." By 1980, the percentages were 2 percent and 23 percent, respectively.[7]

It is worth noting that the trend in attitudes has shifted somewhat since 1980, though the most recent samplings point to a high degree of alienation, as the table below shows.

	1958	1980	1983
Government is run for:			
Benefit of all	82%	23%	34%
Few big interests	18%	77%	66%
Trust the government in Washington to do what is right:			
Always or most of the time	75%	25%	46%
Only some or none of the time	25%	75%	54%

Apathy

Alienation among the mass of average Americans shades off into apathy. Things seem to be going from bad to worse. Nothing we do seems to matter, so why try to do anything? Nowhere does our apathy show up more dramatically than in our voting record.

Of those qualified to vote in the 1982 Congressional elections, 48.5 percent actually did so. In fact, fewer than two-thirds even bothered to register.

It is well known, of course, that voting rates in "off-year" elections are lower than when we are electing a president. And yet, our presidential election record is nothing to brag about. In 1980, in the face of a clear ideological choice between Reagan and Carter, enlivened by the third party candidacy of John Anderson, only 59.2 of the electorate voted.

Voting rates, moreover, are on the decline. Here are some recent figures:[8]

PERCENT OF ELIGIBLE VOTERS VOTING		
Year	Presidential	Off-year
1964	69.3%	
1966		55.4%
1968	67.8%	
1970		54.6%
1972	63.0%	
1974		44.7%
1976	59.2%	
1978		45.9%
1980	59.2%	

Chicago's 1983 mayoral election offered a rare exception to the recent pattern of low voter turnouts. Faced with the choice between electing its first Republican mayor in fifty years or its first black mayor ever, 90 percent of Chicago's voters went to the polls to choose between Bernard Epton and Harold Washington. No one interpreted the high turnout as civic pride or good citizenship, however, and political observers generally agreed that the campaign had been one of the dirtiest in recent memory—with heavy doses of racial issues and even outright racism from both sides.

Journalist Melvin Maddocks has summed up modern American alienation and apathy as well as anyone:

. . . we no longer believe in heroes, but this is not precisely it. Our disbelief runs deeper: We no longer believe in the efficacy of the great deed. For the opposite of heroism is not anti-heroism but helplessness.

How much more powerless we feel as citizens! We doubt that it makes any difference if we vote. We doubt that it makes any difference if we burn unleaded gas or turn down our thermostats. We wonder if anything we do makes any difference—any difference at all.

Our question is not: Can we slay the dragon and rescue the princess? But: What does it matter? Would things really change?[9]

Cynicism

The alienation, disenchantment, and apathy that increasingly characterize modern American life are joined by cynicism. No matter how good or admirable a human act may first appear, we are sure there's something rotten under the surface. This seems due to a perversion of skepticism into cynicism.

The rise of cynicism within the media and among intellectuals can be understood in terms of the reward structure they operate within. Suppose you are a newspaper reporter, and your city editor has assigned you to cover a local businessman who has announced he will give all his money to charity. Inevitably, a question arises as to whether the apparent altruism is genuine or if it is a ruse, hiding some kind of trickery. Your job is to investigate the situation and write a major piece on it. What kind of story are you likely to write? Let's look at the possibilities.

To simplify matters (as we tend to do), let's assume that the businessman's promise is genuine or it's a sham. By the same token, let's assume that your article can either report the act as genuinely altruistic or you can show it to be ingenuine. When these two sets of possibilities are combined, they create a deadly reward structure:

The truth of the offer

Genuine   Sham

	Genuine	Ho hum	New occupation
What you report	Sham	Forgotten	Pulitzer

Let's examine each of the four cells of the table. In the upper-left corner, what would happen if you wrote a positive article and it turned out that the businessman's act was genuinely altruistic? Chances are your article would appear on page 32 of the "Lifestyle" section of the Sunday paper. Your editor might say you show "promise" and should try your hand at "serious" journalism.

Alternatively, let's suppose your article is pretty cynical, suggesting that the businessman is actually working a tax angle, looking for a civic award, or both—but it later turns out that his act was apparently genuine. I use the terms "later turns out" and "apparently" deliberately, since they point to an important distinction between the businessman's act being genuine or false. If it's all a sham, that can become clear suddenly and pretty definitely, with the discovery of a secret Swiss bank account, the publication of a damning letter from the businessman to his accountant, etc. No sudden turn of events can demonstrate the act to be genuine, however. We decide it was genuine when it fails over time to turn out ingenuine. More likely, we simply forget about it altogether. Thus, your cynical article is likely to fade from memory along with the act itself.

So far, it's pretty much a wash. As long as the businessman's act turns out to have been genuinely altruistic, your career as a reporter is not likely to be affected much if you report his act as genuine or suggest it's a sham. But let's look at the more exciting possibilities. Suppose the businessman is really running a con by pretending to give all his money to charity.

If you are taken in by the con and write an article praising him for his altruism, and if the competing newspaper publishes the businessman's letters to his accountant and prints a photocopy of his secret Swiss bank account, and the businessman flees the country two steps ahead of the federal agents, you will not have a long career in journalism. After all, as a journalist you carry a public trust to protect us all from the charlatans, and you have failed. From now on, your career in newspapers is unlikely to progress much beyond selling them.

But what if you had unearthed the damning letters, the bank book, and other evidence of the charade? Pulitzer City. From now on, your biggest professional problem would be living up to your substantial reputation.

It doesn't take a Ph.D. in logic to recognize that the reward structure in effect here is loaded heavily in favor of a negative article. It's not so much that journalists become cynical because of all the evil they've witnessed; being cynical has great survival value.

Everything I've said about journalists applies equally to academics, except academics have a more leisurely deadline to meet. Scholars, like journalists, are charged with the responsibility to protect the rest of us from fakery, and the biggest rewards lie in uncovering ingenuineness, the greatest penalties in overlooking it. It is almost impossible not to look for the worst.

If things weren't bad enough already, the various factors that we've been looking at have a tendency to reinforce each other. The more things are a particular way, the more they get that way. In a related phenomenon, we are at the mercy of "self-fulfilling prophecies."

To the extent that we assume that everyone is out for number one, for example, the more that becomes true. From the standpoint of someone who might want to perform a genuinely altruistic act, to make a genuine contribution, the prospect of cynical scrutiny is a powerful deterrent.

And yet, despite all the powerful reasons for not taking responsibility for public ills, individual Americans do step forth.

Counterpoint: Voluntary Associations

A hundred and fifty years ago, a French aristocrat, Alexis de Tocqueville, toured the still-new United States to discover for himself what kind of society had been created in the New World. Generally despairing of the results of the French Revolution, de Tocqueville warned, "The danger that faces democratic governments is the passivity of the populace; the tendency for individuals to abandon their personal responsibility for social actions." He was generally encouraged by what he discovered in America. In particular, he was struck by the American pattern of forming voluntary associations to deal with public problems. Whatever the public need—building a road or library, repairing a damaged schoolhouse, hiring a community physician—Americans joined together voluntarily to get the job done.

"Volunteering" is still a fundamental part of American life. In a 1981 Gallup poll, for example, 29 percent of the adults surveyed said they were involved in "charity or social service activities, such as helping the poor, the sick, or the elderly." In 1974, the U.S. Bureau of the Census had found 23.5 percent engaged in volunteer work, and the Bureau estimated the value of that work at *over 67 billion dollars.* A 1981 survey by the Roper Organization found a similarly high level of participation:

During the last month:

Contributed money to a charitable
    organization 60%
Gave gifts "in kind" like food,
    furniture, or clothes. 42%

Volunteered your services directly 25%
Worked on a committee or board of a
     charitable organization 13%
Solicited funds for a charitable
     organization 11%

Not only do Americans volunteer, but they see volunteering as essential to American life. Fully 85 percent of those surveyed by Roper agreed that "Even if there is enough money to pay people to provide services, it is still important for community life that a lot of useful work be done by volunteers." And nearly three-fourths *disagreed* with the view that "Volunteer work really isn't respected in this society."

Even during hard economic times, Americans continue to make massive financial contributions to charities. In 1980, corporations and foundations each contributed around 2.5 billion dollars. Individual Americans contributed *40 billion dollars.* [10]

Again, we are left with two faces of American society. On the one hand, we find increasing social complexity robbing individuals of the sense of public responsibility and ownership. People are alienated, disenchanted, cynical, and apathetic. Yet there remains a strong commitment to rise above such feelings and participate fully anyway.

In the chapter that follows, we are going to look more deeply into the kinds of individuals who have demonstrated a willingness to take a stand for excellence. We are about to meet some modern heroes.

4. INDIVIDUALS TAKING CHARGE

The chosen heroes of this earth have been in a minority.
There is not a social, political, or religious privilege that you
enjoy today that was not bought for you by the blood and
tears and patient suffering of the minority. It is the minority
that have stood in the van of every moral conflict, and
achieved all that is noble in the history of the world.
—John Bartholomew Gough

As we've seen, there are powerful forces that can keep ordinary individuals from "meddling" in public affairs. Despite countless opportunities every day to get involved, to take charge of social problems, we've all learned to "mind our own business." Fortunately for all of us, however, there are many brave souls among us who refuse to succumb to those conditions. Some make it their business to step in whenever they disagree with the way things are; others play along until they can't take it any longer.

All of us have our opportunities for heroism. Some of us take those opportunities, others don't. This chapter salutes some of those who have risen to the opportunity for greatness. Some of the heroes we'll consider are people you've heard of, others will be strangers to you. Yet each of them offers proof that individuals like you and me can take on public problems and make a difference in the quality of life for everyone.

Liberty and Justice for All

On December 1, 1955, Rosa Parks, a Montgomery seamstress, was riding the city bus home after a hard day's work. In Alabama at that time, blacks were required to sit in a special section in the back of the bus, and that's what Mrs. Parks was doing. As the bus became more crowded and the "white section" was filled, the bus driver ordered Mrs. Parks and three other blacks to give up their seats to whites just getting on the bus.

Now it's worth noting that Rosa Parks was not responsible for segregation in the South; she didn't create the system, nor was it her job to address the issue. Clearly, that was a job for the nation's lawmakers. Right or wrong, segregation was the law, and no one would have thought the less of an unknown black seamstress for going along with the system.

And yet Rosa Parks didn't give up her seat. She simply refused and in so doing took a stand for human rights that sparked a revolution in black-white relations in America. The opportunity for heroism appeared, and Rosa Parks took it.

Mrs. Parks's refusal and her immediate arrest drew national attention to the situation prevailing in Alabama, showing other blacks that it was possible to challenge the system. Her act of courage that December day set the stage for countless acts of heroism in the years to come.

Montgomery blacks chose to dramatize their outrage at Mrs. Parks's arrest by staging a nonviolent boycott of the city bus system. Leadership for the boycott fell to the black clergy of Montgomery. A new minister in town, Dr. Martin Luther King, Jr., was selected to organize the one-day boycott. No one had any special skills or training for the job, but someone had to do it. King agreed to be the one.

To the surprise of everyone—black and white alike—the boycott was virtually total. Montgomery's black citizens formed car pools, walked to work, rode bicycles—anything but rode the buses. Blacks were organizing their own system of race relations. The boycott continued. Soon the white establishment felt the need to act. Car-pool drivers were harassed and ticketed by police. And the boycott continued. King and other boycott leaders were put in jail. Yet the boycott continued.

The white resistance grew more violent and drew international attention to the boycott, and support for the blacks in Montgomery came from around the world. In November 1956, the black vision of equal treatment took on the force of law when the U.S. Supreme Court ruled that the segregation of buses was unconstitutional.

The heroism of Rosa Parks, Martin Luther King, Jr., and the others who took a stand for human rights created a sharp break in history. None of them had had special training for the job they took on, nor was heroism expected of them. All they had in their favor was the willingness and courage to step out of line and take a stand.

For Martin Luther King, Jr., that December first in Montgomery marked the turning point in his life. From that day on, his life was devoted to personal responsibility for American public life. Now the concern was not just for blacks but for all human beings. In the last years of his life, he would take on the cause of ending the war in Vietnam. Injustice in any form or color was to be challenged. King's courage was to earn him attacks on his character, governmental violation of his privacy, physical assault, jail—and the 1964 Nobel Prize for Peace.

On April 3, 1968, Martin Luther King, Jr., gave his final public speech in Memphis. He had been warned that he would be killed in Memphis. King chose to go anyway, and part of his speech concerned death and also his vision for the possibilities open to humans:

> It doesn't really matter with me now, because I have been to the mountaintop. And I've looked over, and I've seen the promised land. I may not get there with you. But I want you to know that we as a people will get to the

promised land. So I'm happy tonight. I'm not worried about anything. I'm not fearing any man.[1]

On April 4, 1968, Martin Luther King, Jr., was shot and killed.

The civil rights movement of the 1950s and 1960s provides countless examples of real heroism. For some individuals, their heroism cost them physical injury and even death. On March 25, 1964, for example, Viola Liuzzo, a civil rights worker from Chicago, was shot and killed by terrorists on the highway between Montgomery and Selma. Many others paid the same price. Other heroes of the civil rights movement were imprisoned, others suffered financially, and many suffered disapproval from family and friends.

At the same time, each person who dedicated his or her life to the civil rights movement demonstrated the power of individuals to change the course of history. Sometimes, a relatively small act of courage made a dramatic statement.

On May 4, 1961, an integrated group of thirteen "Freedom Riders" boarded a bus in Washington, D.C., for the purpose of testing the desegregation of public facilities between Washington and New Orleans. Their troubles began in the town of Anniston, Alabama.

Anniston, the seat for Calhoun County in northeastern Alabama, lies about fifty miles from Birmingham. It was first established as a private company town in 1872 for the manufacture of iron and textiles, and became a public town in 1883. Originally named Woodstock after the Woodstock Iron Company, it was later renamed after the company president's wife, Annie. This was clearly a town that looked after its own affairs and didn't feel it needed any interference from outsiders.

Five miles outside of Anniston, the Freedom bus was forced to the side of the road by a mob of three hundred to four hundred angry whites. The bus driver was allowed to leave the bus, locking the door as he did so, thus offering a minimum degree of protection to the riders.

Unable to get inside, the mob began beating on the bus and threatening to kill the riders. After about five minutes, some form of incendiary device was thrown into the bus, and it began sparking, smoking, and burning. At first, the Freedom Riders chose to take their chances on the bus, since the mob outside looked like sudden death. Eventually, the smoke and fire in the bus was too much to take, and they began stumbling off the bus.

Outside the bus, the people of Anniston, dressed in their Sunday best for Mother's Day, began beating the riders with baseball bats, driving them to the ground, and kicking them. When someone yelled, "The bus is going to explode!" the mob pulled back a bit, and the Freedom Riders were left broken and bleeding, their throats parched and lungs filled with smoke from the fire.

A twelve-year-old white girl, Janie Forsythe, had witnessed the attack from her front yard. The bus had been stopped and set fire right in front of her house. She had stood helpless as the mob brutalized the passengers getting off the bus. Now she stood among the white onlookers, watching the victims gasping and coughing.

Bolting from the crowd of onlookers, Janie ran into her house, filled a bucket with water, and returned outside with a stack of paper cups. Forcing her way through the crowd, she ran to the bus riders and gave them water. For the next several minutes, she ran back and forth between the brutalized Freedom Riders and her kitchen, getting more water for them as her neighbors watched in disbelief.

The most support Janie received from the mob was one man who defended her action by saying, "Hell, you'd give a dog water." Twenty years later, Janie would recall that as the day she decided to leave the South. In her judgment, she hadn't done much for the Freedom Riders, but it was all she could see to do. More important, she was the only one willing to take any humane action that day in Anniston. Twenty years later, the Freedom Riders would remember Janie fondly as their only ray of hope that day. A caring twelve-year-old girl showed once more that heroism takes many forms and fits any size of human being.

Crime in the Streets

In recent years, no social problem has been more terrifying to city dwellers than the danger of street violence. Rape, muggings, and senseless beatings have become an unhappy staple of urban living. In 1982, half of those questioned in a national survey said there was an area within a mile of home where they would be afraid to walk alone at night. One person in seven did not feel safe at home at night.[2]

Most Americans handle the problem of violence in an individualistic fashion. We stay home at night. We avoid dangerous areas when we can. We never travel alone if we can help it. And in 1982, half the nation's adult population said they had a gun at home.

In 1979, one young man took a different approach to the problem of street violence. Curtis Sliwa, a McDonald's manager, persuaded twelve friends to join him in riding the New York subways at night. Calling themselves the Magnificent Thirteen, Sliwa and his friends announced to the public that they were prepared to intervene and break up rapes, muggings, and other acts of violence. As others expressed interest in joining, the group expanded and was renamed the Guardian Angels.

The specific purpose of the Guardian Angels is to create a "visual deterent" to violent crime. To accomplish that, each Angel is trained in self-defense techniques, first aid, and the law. Traveling in patrols of six to ten members, their distinctive red berets and white T-shirts announce that any acts of violence in the vicinity will be challenged and stopped. The point of the patrols is not to engage in street battles with thugs but to keep violence from happening in the first place. In the words of Lester Dixon, former head of the San Francisco chapter, "The most successful patrol is one where nothing happens."

Here's a good example of how the Guardian Angels work. I

had arranged to participate in a training session one Monday night in San Francisco. After a rigorous physical workout, we gathered on a staircase for a rap session on racial attitudes. In the midst of the discussion, two young thugs had the bad sense to try mugging an old man just outside the door. Suddenly, fifteen to twenty Guardian Angels poured out onto the street.

Now you might take a minute to imagine what would have transpired on the street that night. My guess is that you'll imagine something akin to a Bruce Lee movie. Nothing could have been farther from the truth.

The first Angel out the door was an eighteen-year-old black named Fred. As he approached the situation, Fred thought he recognized one of the young thugs. "Hey, blood, what's coming down?" Soon, Fred and the other Angels were in a conversation with the two thugs, talking them out of the mugging, and separating them from the old man. In a matter of minutes, the situation just wound down to nothing. The Angels sat the old man down in the doorway by our meeting and called him a cab.

Response to the Guardian Angels has varied widely in cities across the country. In New York, where the Angels originated, they were first condemned by the city government, then later accepted. When San Francisco turned a cold shoulder to the Angels, San Jose invited them to come south.

In 1981, I had an opportunity to go on patrol with the San Francisco Angels and witness the grassroots response firsthand. Coming to an intersection, we paused to let a bus pass by. When the driver saw the patrol, he began blowing his horn and waving. At first, I attributed this to the fact that Lester Dixon was a San Francisco bus driver. But then, we had the same experience with a passing firetruck, with all the firemen leaning over to wave. Police on their beats were equally friendly and supportive. Lester suggested why that was so.

"The police have a really rough job out here. They're expected to keep the streets safe, and yet they don't get much respect or support. They know we're here to support them, not to take their jobs away."

Walking through the financial district, we were stopped by a gentleman in a three-piece suit, who crossed the street to say, "I just wanted to shake your hand and thank you for being here." The response was the same everywhere we went that day.

Dixon explained that resistance to the Angels seemed to come from two quarters. On the one hand, city officials sometimes resisted the Angels because their very presence seemed to suggest that the government was unable to keep peace on the streets. Moreover, there was a concern that official approval of the Angels might make the city financially liable in the event that anything went wrong. That resistance seemed to be weakening, however, as the Angels demonstrated that they were preventing trouble rather than causing it.

The other source of resistance came from street people. At the beginning, many feared that the Angels were moral vigilantes come to hassle pot-smokers and prostitutes. This image may have come from the strict no-dope, no-alcohol rules for Angels on patrol. (Anyone who arrives for a patrol with alcohol on his or her breath, for example, is no longer a Guardian Angel.) Over time, however, the street people have come to realize that the Angels have one purpose and one purpose only —to prevent violence.

People who have only heard about the Guardian Angels at second hand often wonder why they do it. Nobody gets paid for being an Angel. Moreover, the training is demanding, and the work is time-consuming. Being a Guardian Angel often means walking the streets in the cold and the rain, risking injury and death. Yet the question of why they do it is answered in just a few minutes of any patrol.

Usually young, often from an ethnic minority, the typical Guardian Angel would have little opportunity to make a real contribution in the normal course of things. Nobody asks these young people what they think. They are unlikely to be chosen to serve on boards of directors or asked to run for public office. Yet every Guardian Angel on the street knows he or she is making a real contribution, one that is appreciated and respected. By taking on personal responsibility for public safety, they have created their own opportunity for heroism. By early 1984, around four thousand Guardian Angels were patrolling the streets, buses, and subways of nearly fifty cities in the United States, Canada, and Puerto Rico.

Community Boards

Other individuals have tackled the problem of crime from a different direction. For Raymond Shonholtz, a San Francisco attorney, it all began when he was asked to direct a 1975 task force of attorneys for the California Assembly Committee on Criminal Justice considering a revision of the state's penal code. Some of the issues being addressed were the general logjam of cases before the courts, the problems that had arisen in connection with inaeterminate sentencing, a desire to route juveniles out of the system whenever possible, and the general feeling that the criminal justice system didn't work.

In the course of his research, Shonholtz uncovered a few innovative programs in other countries that used panels of citizens to do the work normally done by judges and juries. Typically, panels of laypeople heard and handled cases under the general guidance of a magistrate. For example, Norway had such a program for alcoholics; Scotland had one for juvenile cases. The more he thought about the citizen panels against the backdrop of problems facing the American criminal justice system, the more he began to envision the possibility of profound reforms in the execution of justice.

In Shonholtz's eyes, the citizen panels represented much more than a mere convenience. In 1982, he explained a part of his viewpoint this way: "One of the key reasons why there is plea-bargaining in the modern urban court is not because the court's overburdened; the primary reason is because victims don't participate in their cases." Once a crime has been committed, a process begins that transforms the crime into something far removed from the actual situation where it occurred and far removed from the people affected by it. And the victims were not the only principals removed from the case. Shonholtz commented on the origins and evolution of the jury system:

> The origin of the Anglo-Saxon model of a jury was a far, far cry from what it currently is. The idea of having a deaf, dumb, and blind jury—which is currently what we have —would be a total anomaly to the early formation of the Anglo-Saxon jury. They were people who, by law, *had* to know the defendants or parties, had to be familiar with the situation, had to be familiar with the locale—and even as the industrial age moved on, those factors held for a long, long time. If you didn't know something, you were disqualified.

Over time, the jury system evolved to embrace the view that fairness could best be achieved through ignorance of the case. Jurors were to reach their verdicts on the basis of what was presented in court and nothing more. In the process, the jury, and the court system with it, became separated from the neighborhoods where the crimes occurred, separated from the people most directly involved.

The result of Shonholtz's research and thinking was something called "community boards." Here's an illustration of how they work. Let's suppose you and I are next-door neighbors in an urban community. Suppose further that you have a dog that barks all night. If you and I were "normal" modern neighbors, I might politely ask you to do something about it. If that didn't work, I would probably put up with the dog's barking for as long as I could. Once my rage grew too great to contain, I might start yelling out my window: "Shut that goddamn dog up or else!" When that didn't work, matters might progress in any number of directions. I might start throwing things at the dog or at your windows. If I could get your phone number, I might start calling you in the middle of the night to complain. Maybe I'd call the police. Or, if I were so inclined, I might get a gun and shoot your dog—or worse. The chances are pretty good that one or both of us would end up in court, and whatever came of that probably wouldn't solve the original problem or any of those that followed from it.

Now let's suppose that we lived in a community with a community board. I might begin by asking you to stop your dog from barking, and if that failed to produce a result, I would drop in at the community board office. There, I would tell a staff member (possibly a volunteer from the neighborhood) about my problem with your dog. Subsequently, someone from the community board office (again, possibly a volunteer) would visit you to discuss the problem. There's a good chance that a solution to the problem would be discovered at that point. If not, you would be invited—with me—to attend a community board panel meeting of our neighbors to work the problem out. Though you couldn't be forced to appear before the panel, that would be presented as an alternative to my taking the matter to the police and the courts.

Suppose you agreed to appear before the panel. One evening, you and I would come to a meeting room in the neighborhood —perhaps in a church or a community organization's building —to discuss our problem with a panel of, say, five of our neighbors. I would begin by describing the problem from my point of view. You could then present your side of the matter. The members of the panel would begin participating in the discussion, asking questions for clarification and encouraging us to find a mutually satisfactory solution.

Purposely, the panel members would not suggest solutions. Unlike a jury, they would not reach a decision. Rather, their purpose would be to assist you and me in finding our own solution. If we were successful—the chances are better than nine in ten that we would be—the panel would work with us further in getting our agreement clarified and specified so as to avoid any later ambiguities. Thus, you agree to bring your dog inside the house every evening by ten P.M. and keep it there, and I agree to stop throwing rocks at your windows.

Once the agreement had been sufficiently specified, it would be typed up for signatures: yours, mine, and the panel members'. In addition, we would work out a method of follow-up and enforcement. Perhaps a community board member would arrange to call us the first few Fridays to see if the solution was working.

All this would be accomplished outside the court system, with an opportunity to explore different facets of the situation without the constraints of "rules of evidence" and an ability to discover whatever solutions would work without reference to legally prescribed remedies. The matter would have been resolved by those people most directly affected by it: our neighbors.

It is important to realize that, while the panel members are trained in conflict resolution, they have no training in the law, no expertise in the criminal justice system. Shonholtz was determined from the beginning that the panels be comprised of true "peers." In creating the first panels, in fact, Shonholtz was careful to avoid "community leaders": no clergy, no attorneys, etc. Rather than the chairperson of the local community association, Shonholtz looked for the person who arrived early to set up the chairs, make the coffee, and who stayed afterward to clean up after a meeting. As he met such people in a neighborhood, he invited them to form a community board and then trained them in conflict resolution.

In the context of this book, it is worth considering some of the problems Shonholtz had to deal with in order to establish community boards as functioning, effective bodies in San Francisco neighborhoods.

1. Finding individuals who would be suitable members for panels.
2. Explaining the idea of community boards to those people.

3. Persuading them that they should give up substantial amounts of their time to be trained in conflict resolution and then to serve on panels.

4. Getting the residents of a neighborhood to bring their grievances to the community board rather than to the courts.

5. Persuading those in the official criminal justice system that the community boards were a positive contribution to the system rather than a threat to it.

How Shonholtz overcame each of these obstacles is less important than our realizing that the success of the community board movement depended on his willingness and commitment to overcome them. As of early 1984, community boards had been established in twenty-one San Francisco neighborhoods and six other cities across the country. Shonholtz estimates that eleven to twelve hundred residents have been trained in conflict resolution, and more are being trained all the time—including some fourth- and fifth-grade classes in the San Francisco schools.

During 1983, 550 cases were heard by community board panels in San Francisco, 86 percent of which resulted in written resolutions. Virtually all the others were settled informally, without written resolutions. All these successes have depended on ordinary citizens taking on personal responsibility for public problems.

Making a Difference in Prison

For anyone who feels that their life situation doesn't offer them an opportunity for heroism, doesn't really offer them a chance to make a difference, the stories of three prisoners should be especially instructive. Stanley Fletcher, Robert Frogge, and Sidney Rittenberg each created his own opportunity under unlikely circumstances.

Serving a fifty-year sentence in a Texas prison for two counts of rape, Stanley Fletcher could easily have written his life off as being of no significance.[3] After ten years in prison, however,

Fletcher's life took a new downturn when he learned that his youngest son, Curtis, had held up a Houston woman with a shotgun and was facing a nine-year prison sentence. Fletcher had known his children were frequently getting in trouble, and he blamed the problem on his absence from the home—compounded by the bad example he had set. Fletcher described his feelings to reporter, Arnold Hamilton:

> With their daddy in prison, I guess it was pretty hard for a woman to properly see that all six were attended to. If I had been there, I'm convinced not one of the boys would have strayed. It like to drove me crazy the first four or five years I was down here. I was worrying myself sick they'd start fooling with alcohol or drugs and end up here. As it was, their mother wouldn't let me correspond with them. I was of no influence at all.

Fletcher's dilemma was by no means unusual. He was not the only father in prison watching his children go bad. Most handle their problem by complaining that it isn't their fault or by submerging themselves in guilt. Fletcher chose a different response for himself. Pulling together what little influence he had with prison officials, he began working to have Curtis sentenced to his prison. After months of effort, he succeeded, and father and son became cellmates. The elder Fletcher then began teaching his son carpentry and encouraging the fourth-grade dropout to complete a high-school diploma. Stanley Fletcher had created his own opportunity for heroism.

I first met Robert Frogge in 1976 at San Quentin, where he was serving a life sentence with no possibility of parole. I was visiting San Quentin, Lompoc, and Leavenworth to interview prisoners who had taken the est training, a program aimed at personal transformation and mastery in life. Prior to arriving at San Quentin, I had been told Robert was an unusual prisoner, and my own experience confirmed it.

Frogge's first brush with the law came in 1961 while he was

serving in the Air Force. Stealing a car and firearms, he went AWOL to Mexico, where he was apprehended. After an Air Force prison term, Frogge was kicked out of the service.

Returning home to Indiana, Frogge married and had a child who died at ten weeks of age. From that time on, his life turned increasingly to crime. Frogge and his wife, Sylvia, formed a partnership in armed robbery. After several robberies in Indiana, the couple moved their operations north and were arrested in Milwaukee on Washington's Birthday, 1965.

Frogge was sentenced to ten years in prison in Indiana, but he escaped after only thirteen months. During the next nineteen days, he staged robberies in Indiana, Colorado, and California. California proved his undoing, however. He was arrested in Bakersfield for kidnap/robbery with attempted murder. For his efforts, California rewarded him with a sentence of life without possibility of parole for kidnapping, three separate sentences of five-years-to-life for armed robbery, and one-to-twenty years for attempted murder. In addition, he was taken to San Diego to stand trial for armed robbery there and received an additional sentence of five-years-to-life. To round out his future, Frogge still owed Indiana nine years on his original sentence there, plus another five years for escaping.

Frogge was taken from San Diego to Folsom prison to begin serving the rest of his life behind bars. Given his past history, he was housed in Folsom's maximum security section. In 1968, however, Frogge built a crossbow in the prison hobby shop and attempted to escape. Unsuccessful in the attempt; he was given three years in "the hole."

In 1969, Frogge was transferred from Folsom to San Quentin, where he finished his term in the hole. By the time he returned to a regular cell, Frogge had established an admirable reputation among the other inmates. In his own terms, he was a "successful convict." Not only was he doing life without possibility of parole for heavy crimes, but he had successfully escaped from prison in Indiana and attempted another escape in California.

In November 1971, Frogge was transported to Los Angeles to appear as a witness at a robbery trial. This trip produced another unsuccessful escape attempt. The next year, he planned another escape. Claiming credit for a robbery he didn't actually commit, he was taken to Texas for trial. On the way, he jumped the federal marshal and tried to escape. Again, he was unsuccessful, and he added two more sentences to his record: five years for attempted escape and three years of federal time for assaulting the marshal.

Frogge's final escape attempt came in 1974, when he was taken to Fairfield, California, to appear as a witness in another trial. An inspection of his clothing revealed a set of hacksaw blades, and Frogge was back in the hole for ten days.

Looking back on it all, Frogge describes those ten days as the hardest of his life. They also proved to be a profound turning point for him. For ten days, Frogge reviewed his life, asking himself what life was really about and what he really wanted out of it. He recognized that he had become an absolutely successful convict, admired by all the other inmates, and he realized that it wasn't what he wanted.

Frogge spent the next two years looking at what he wanted out of life. In 1976, his life took some dramatic turns. In June, he began working with other convicts in a program called SQUIRES (San Quentin Utilizations of Inmate Resources, Experiences, and Studies). On three successive Saturdays, the inmates would meet with a group of juvenile delinquents, rapping with them about their problems and counseling them against a life of crime.

At about the same time, Frogge and several other inmates participated in the est training, donated to San Quentin by est. For Frogge, the training clarified and completed his two years of self-examination. He became determined that the remainder of his life would be dedicated to making a contribution to others.

Two months later, California amended the law that had resulted in Frogge's sentence of life without possibility of parole.

On July 1977, when the law took effect, Frogge became eligible for parole. The transformation that had begun during those ten days in the hole had produced a perfect candidate for parole, and Frogge was released from San Quentin on December 29, 1978.

After four days in the Marin County jail on an old contempt of court charge, Frogge was taken to Lompoc Federal Correctional Institute to begin serving his federal time. A model prisoner, he was paroled from Lompoc on December 22, 1980. This time there were no guards, no federal marshals, no new prison to go to. He was truly free for the first time since 1965.

A free man at last, Frogge continued in his commitment to make a contribution. During the summer of 1981, he and his new wife Pamela conceived the idea of creating an organization dedicated to bringing an end to crime. End Crime, Inc., was born with the mission of educating people about crime, supporting them in ending crime in their own lives, and organizing people to bring an end to crime in society. With Pamela as president, the couple began establishing a viable organization in the San Francisco area and spawning similar groups in seven other states.

In addition to working with the general public, Frogge also began a peer counseling program for inmates at San Quentin. One night a week, he returns to the prison where he spent eight years of his life to tell the convicts that there is another way, that it's possible to turn their lives around no matter how bad they've been.

No prison story I know of is more compelling than that of Sidney Rittenberg, an American from Charleston, South Carolina, who went to China with the U.S. Army in 1945. At the Far Eastern Languages School, he had initially planned to study Japanese, but a friend warned him that he was likely to get stuck with the Army of Occupation once the war was over —thus delaying his return home an extra year or two. To guard against that possibility, Rittenberg switched to Chinese, a decision that was to delay his return home for thirty-four years.

Much of Rittenberg's initial work in China involved him as an interpreter in the American attempts to make peace between Chiang Kai-shek's Kuomintang government and the communist insurgents under Mao Tse-tung and Chou En-Lai. This meant that he was able to move freely in areas controlled by both the government and the rebels. The contrast he saw was striking. In the communist areas, he found effective organization and a genuine commitment to the welfare of the people. Students were organized to canvass neighborhoods to find out who was in need, and every bit of food was used carefully to ensure that no one went hungry. Rittenberg was greatly impressed with what he saw, and he eventually became good friends with Chou En-Lai.

In the areas controlled by the Kuomintang, on the other hand, corruption was rampant. Relief shipments of food were quickly channeled into the black market and, on occasions, sold back to the relief agencies. Even in the most productive grain-growing areas, the landscape was littered by corpses of those who had died of hunger.

In 1946, with the completion of his duties in China, Rittenberg booked passage to the United States. Before leaving, he visited Madame Sun Yat-sen to say good-bye. Madame Sun urged Rittenberg to visit Chou En-Lai before leaving China. Chou expressed his dismay at Rittenberg's pending departure and urged him to say good-bye to Mao Tse-tung.

Traveling to North China, Rittenberg found Mao preparing radio broadcasts to the United States aimed at telling the American people the truth about events in China. He asked Rittenberg to stay a little while to correct the English translations of the radio messages. Rittenberg agreed, feeling he would have an opportunity to contribute to improved Chinese-American relations.

Within a month, a full-scale civil war had broken out in China, cutting Rittenberg off from the outside world until the communist victory in 1949. For three years, Rittenberg worked with Mao: translating Chinese documents into English, training translators, and generally educating himself about China. In the process, he was forming a personal commitment to building a bridge between the American and Chinese people.

Rittenberg's vision of making a contribution to U.S.–Chinese relations ran into trouble shortly after the communist revolution in 1949. Stalin was particularly concerned that China be protected from American influences, so his security chief informed Peking that he had proof Rittenberg was a spy. The Chinese were urged to hold him in custody while the evidence was being sent. Soon, Rittenberg was in a Chinese prison, where he was to spent the next six years—most of the time in solitary confinement. His Chinese wife divorced him, and it appeared that Rittenberg's life was essentially over.

At the outset of his imprisonment, Rittenberg was given the option of becoming a double agent. If he confessed to being an American spy and agreed to work for the Chinese, he would be given passage to the United States. The only problem was that Rittenberg knew he wasn't a spy, and he recognized that his false confession would end any possibility of making the contribution he had committed himself to. He chose to stay in prison, protesting for six years that he was not a spy. Ultimately, the evidence of Rittenberg's spying never arrived from Russia, and he was finally released from prison and publicly acknowledged as a friend of the Chinese people.

Put yourself in Rittenberg's shoes for a moment, and you may very well decide this would have been a good time to leave China. Rittenberg had stayed there to make a contribution, and his dedication had been rewarded with betrayal and false imprisonment. For Sidney Rittenberg, however, this seemed like a good time to get back to work, to get on with the job he had created for himself.

One day, as he was reestablishing himself in government service, Rittenberg visited an office to talk about jobs. While he was in the official's inner office, he could hear a heated discussion among the secretaries in the outer office. He was, of course, something of a celebrity, and they were excited to have him visiting their office. One of the women, however, was steadfast in her view that Rittenberg's wife should have stuck by him, that her disloyalty was unforgiveable.

Rittenberg was so taken by the secretary's impassioned speech that he wanted to meet her. Shortly thereafter, Wang Yulin became the second Mrs. Sidney Rittenberg. In the years to come, moreover, she would have an opportunity to test her commitment to a wife's loyalty to her husband.

For the next fourteen years, Rittenberg worked in a variety of capacities in China, all reflecting his determination to improve U.S.–Chinese relations. These were not the best of times for an American in China, however, and in February 1968, in the frenzy of the Cultural Revolution, a carload of soldiers arrived one cold night and took him away from his wife and children. This time, Rittenberg was to spend ten years in prison, all of it in solitary confinement.

It is worth taking a moment to imagine how such an experience might affect you. Totally separated from friends and loved ones, separated from any outside contact, you would sit day after day in the same tiny cell, not knowing when or if you would ever be free again.

For Sidney Rittenberg, the experience drove him back to the fundamentals of life. What was life all about? What really mattered? Certainly not material possessions. Not even friends and family. He had been deprived of all those things we would normally think of as valuable. Ultimately, Rittenberg concluded that "making a contribution" was the ultimate value, knowing that his life made some difference in the events of the planet.

With this in mind, he devoted every day to finding ways of making some small contribution. First, he dedicated himself to keeping his cell spotlessly clean. He used tiny scraps of rags to scrub the cell. When the guards came by periodically with a mop for the prisoners to use on their cells, they found Sidney had no need for it.

Years later, Rittenberg's guards and interrogators would

admit that they had become convinced of his innocence after about six months. He simply did not act like any guilty person they had known. His behavior, his emotions, everything about him corresponded to the dedication and innocence he claimed were true.

Although Rittenberg's guards had been ordered not to communicate with the prisoner, he broke that barrier down bit by bit. Sidney Rittenberg is a master storyteller, now as then. Speaking excellent Chinese, Rittenberg would tell his guards stories about growing up in South Carolina and about life in the United States in general. In all this, he experienced making some small contribution to friendly relations between the two countries—the reason he had stayed in China in the first place.

Such was the nature of Sidney Rittenberg's life for ten long years. In hearing such an account, we are tempted to conclude that Sidney Rittenberg was different from you and me. He must have had some special grace that permitted him to survive with sanity, whereas you and I could not—something Rittenberg denies.

To complete the picture of those ten years, he describes waking up slowly every morning, slowly experiencing the crushing realization that he was still in prison, still in solitary confinement, totally cut off from those he loved, not knowing if he would ever be free. Every morning for ten years, he had to recommit himself to making a contribution.

Rittenberg describes his morning recommitment this way: "I'm not under this stone. I'm not passive. I'm learning something, doing something, thinking about something. I'm going to live on, I'm not going to die." Every morning he recreated the view that prison was something added to his life, a part of his education, not something taken away from life.

Sidney Rittenberg did not and does not possess some ability that others lack. Any of us could have done what he did. What may separate him from others was the *willingness* to do it. Every morning for ten years, he faced the opportunity of being life's victim, knowing that no one could ever criticize him for that. And yet, every morning he chose something else.

After ten years in prison (now a total of sixteen years), Sidney Rittenberg was released with an apology and reinstatement in Chinese society. The man who walked out of prison was healthy, sane, enthusiastic about his life, and ready to go back to work. He had no bitterness over his experience, no need for revenge. For forty years, Sidney Rittenberg's life has been devoted to creating peace and understanding between the Chinese and American people and nations. The years in prison were as much an opportunity to pursue that goal as any other situation. Reunited with his wife, Yulin, Rittenberg now leads Computerland's China program, still determined to make the contribution that has guided most of his adult life.

Consumer Protection

In 1965, a young lawyer shocked the nation with his book, *Unsafe at Any Speed,* which pointed to gross irresponsibility within the automobile industry. In the years that followed, Ralph Nader was to become a household word, making consumer rights and consumer protection an established concern within American society. His efforts have resulted in state and federal legislation and numerous private consumer organizations, including over a hundred campus-based "public interest research groups." Ralph Nader is a true model for the theme of this book: individuals taking personal responsibility for public problems.

More than any particular legislation or organization, however, Nader's greatest contribution lies in having made personal responsibility for public problems available as an option for others in society. Because of his courage and willingness to step forward, many thousands of other Americans have been empowered to do the same. Leslie Hughes, a Rochester, New York, housewife and mother is an example.

After a family outing on October 24, 1982, Hughes and her family stopped at a local McDonald's to get food to take home. They decided to try the new "Happy Meals." This new offering contained both food and toys, such as a rifle-carrying sheriff and a spear-toting Indian.

Hughes describes what happened after dinner. "I took the toys out of the box and I couldn't believe it. The rifle was so small that my daughter could have put it in her ear or her nose or her mouth. My husband and I agreed that these weren't for small children. It really surprised me that McDonald's would give these things out."

Any "normal," responsible mother would have thrown the toys away and resolved not to buy any more. An even more responsible mother might have warned her friends about the potential danger. Leslie Hughes went even further. A member of the Empire State Consumer Association, she called the group's president, Judy Braiman-Lipson, and suggested she look into the matter.

Braiman-Lipson purchased her own Happy Meals and conducted a few tests of her own, inserting the rifle into a cylinder about the size of her daughter's throat. She was sufficiently concerned by what she learned that she called the Rochester representative of McDonald's, who agreed to set up a conference call with the United States Testing Co., the firm who had tested the toys for safety. In addition, she called the U.S. Consumer Product Safety Commission in Washington, and the federal government got into the act. A CPSC official visited a Washington McDonald's and asked for samples. Government testing began.

In addition to the danger posed by the small size of the rifles and spears, the government inspectors found that young children could easily break off the arms and legs of the figures, creating something more to swallow and choke on. The CPSC informed McDonald's of the results of their initial tests.

On Halloween night, just a week after the Hughes family outing, a group of twenty McDonald's executives met to discuss the crisis. After a four-hour meeting, they called the CPSC chairman and arranged a meeting in Washington for the next day.

On November 1, the CPSC revealed the latest results of their testing to the McDonald's executives. The toys were clearly unsafe for children three and under. By noon, representatives of the Schaper Manufacturing Co., the firm who manufactured the toys for McDonald's, arrived in Washington. They suggested labeling the toys as only suitable for children four and older. McDonald's chose instead to withdraw the toys altogether. Early that evening, conferences calls were being made throughout the McDonald's chain, and all the toys had been withdrawn by midnight.

I've drawn out the details of this story for a purpose. On the one hand, I want to acknowledge the complexity of the problems we face in modern society. This is the complexity that often keeps us from taking action. The withdrawal of the toys in this case required actions by hundreds, perhaps thousands of people. At the same time, I want to make it clear that all those actions began with the willingness of one woman to speak out and take a stand. Anyone could have done it. Leslie Hughes did.

5. AN IDEA WHOSE TIME HAS COME

There is one thing stronger than all the armies in the world: and that is an idea whose time has come.

—*Victor Hugo*

In chapter 4 we've seen that, despite social pressure to the contrary, many individuals have been willing to take on personal responsibility for public problems ranging from the seemingly trivial to the global. While the courageous acts we've been examining are the acts of *individuals,* it's important that we see those individual acts of heroism in a larger context. Indeed, they are an integral part of perhaps the most powerful force on earth: *an idea whose time has come.* [1]

Solving Big Problems

In examining some of the problems that plague the world—hunger, overpopulation, war, to name a few—we often look to technology for solutions. Better crop strains, we think, will end the ages-old tragedy of starvation. Better contraceptive techniques will stop the ticking of the population bomb. Couldn't war be prevented if only we had weapons that everyone agreed were too terrible to ever use? Many people have believed these things in the past, and many still do. Yet, despite major breakthroughs on each of these fronts, the problems persist.

Impressive developments in the "green revolution" have greatly increased agricultural productivity on the planet, yet 13 to 18 million people still die of hunger each year. The condom did not end the population explosion; neither did the diaphragm, birth control pills, vasectomies, or any of the other birth control methods that have been developed and improved over the years. By the same token, there were those who once believed that the tank was so horrible an engine of war that nations would never fight again. They were wrong. So were those who believed the machine gun was too terrible a weapon to be used. Nor have the horrors of thermonuclear war kept nations at peace. In sum, technology has not saved us the way people have hoped it would.

Indeed, technology has produced as many problems as it has solved. In fact, the solution to one problem (DDT to kill insects, for instance) often *becomes* a problem in its own right later on (e.g., residual poisons showing up in milk). Similarly, innovations in public sanitation in some developing countries have initially lowered death rates, resulting in rapid population growth, causing food shortages, and ultimately producing higher death rates than ever before.

Even though technology has not solved all our problems the way we have often hoped, we human beings have actually eliminated some of our major problems, even problems that seemed inevitable to people beforehand. The elimination of slavery is a good example.

At the beginning of the nineteenth century, an airtight case could have been made for the inevitability of slavery. After all, some people would always be more powerful than others, and slavery was an obvious outcome, as history documented. In the United States, it was obvious to many people that the nation's economy would collapse without slavery. Furthermore, the institution was three hundred years old in America; something like that couldn't be changed.

It could be argued, moreover, that the slaves themselves

depended on the institution of slavery. If they were set free, they wouldn't know how to care for themselves. Even the Bible seemed to suggest that God intended that some of his children live out their worldly existence as slaves. Many well-meaning people argued that the goal should be to make slavery more humane.

Despite all these powerful reasons for the inevitability of slavery, it essentially vanished from the earth during the nineteenth century. When we look back on the elimination of slavery on the planet, we often explain its passing as the embodiment of an idea whose time had come.

Probably the same will be said about the elimination of other major problems sometime in the future. People have been aware of the problem of overpopulation at least since the time of Malthus. Awareness of the problem reached a new high during the 1960s and 1970s, though the problem was not ended. Even though people still debate the current seriousness of the problem, no one denies that population growth must end sometime. There is a point at which the mass of human bodies would cause the planet to collapse into itself. Well in advance of that, however, the life-support systems of the planet would be exhausted. Clearly, population growth will cease eventually. When it does, moreover, we will say that it finally became an idea whose time had come. The same will be said about the eventual elimination of world hunger.

It seems clear to me that eventually men and women will enjoy truly equal opportunity in America. We are currently in the midst of the process that will have that outcome. Sometime in the future, people will look back on our times and regard sexual inequality with a certain degree of disbelief that things really were this way. "But how could they continue year after year, paying men almost twice as much as they paid women?" Some will be horrified, regarding us the way we now regard the Salem witch-burners. Others in that future generation will find our exclusion of women from certain occupations (and men from others) as sort of amusing, the way we regard colonial "blue laws" that prohibited dancing on the Sabbath. For all but a reactionary few, however, equality will be regarded as the obvious and natural state of affairs.

Whenever true sexual equality is finally achieved in America, people will explain the shift by saying it was an idea whose time had come. All these observations point directly at a vital question facing us today: How do you cause an idea's time to come?

Causing an Idea's Time to Come

For all our technological developments, we do not know how to *cause* an idea's time to come. Until we can answer that question, we are fated to continue suffering our major social problems until circumstances seemingly beyond our control do away with them.

Even if we aren't really sure how to cause an idea's time to come, it has happened from time to time. Perhaps the best recent example is the eradication of smallpox. Most contemporary Americans have little awareness of this age-old killer, but Philip Boffey puts it in this historical perspective:

> Some experts contend that smallpox, by some measures, has been the most fearsome scourge in human experience, causing more harm over a longer period and in more geographic areas than such other forms of pestilence as bubonic plague, cholera, and yellow fever. The devastation it once caused was illustrated by an epidemic that killed 31 percent of the population of Iceland in 1707. As recently as 1926 an international conference was told that smallpox could be found in virtually every country.[2]

In 1967, the World Health Organization launched a worldwide campaign to eradicate the disease. Their objective was the total annihilation of the virus on the planet. On August 9, 1977, the last known case of smallpox was recorded in Somalia. During the years that followed, the United Nations offered a reward of one thousand dollars to anyone who reported another case.

No one collected the reward, and in 1979 smallpox was officially declared to be ended. The victory over smallpox had been achieved through the efforts of 600 health officials and some 150,000 to 200,000 health workers around the world.

In 1967, an air-tight case could have been made for the inevitability of smallpox. After all, there were over 4 billion people in the world, many of them living in abominable poverty in faraway corners of the earth. How could all of them be protected from the disease?

In some areas, the people had superstitious fears about innoculation. Others had firm religious prohibitions against it. In some countries, dictatorial rulers were not willing to have UN workers roaming the countryside. Once the commitment was made to eradicate smallpox, however, a powerful shift of context occurred. What was once a reason why smallpox couldn't be eradicated now became an obstacle on the road to eradicating it. The many obstacles were overcome in many ways, just as slavery was eliminated through a variety of methods.

Those WHO officials who gathered in 1967 to make a commitment to the eradication of smallpox were creating an idea whose time had come. What they created was far more powerful than any technological breakthroughs in medicine. It is worth noting that though some advances had been made in the storing and administration of the vaccine, smallpox was finally eradicated through the use of a vaccine invented 150 years ago.

The elimination of smallpox illustrates the possibility of consciously and deliberately causing an idea's time to come. The American space program that resulted in the landing of three astronauts on the moon in 1969 offers another example. At the time that President John F. Kennedy declared the nation's commitment to reach the moon by the end of the sixties, powerful arguments were made to prove the impossibility of space travel, and yet we did it.

The Role of Individuals

Whatever else it may take to cause an idea's time to come, one thing seems clear: it cannot happen without individual initiative and responsibility. Somewhere in the history of any idea's time coming, we will find at least one individual taking a stand; usually we find more than one.

The American civil rights movement was clearly an idea whose time had come. At the same time, it cannot be separated from Rosa Parks's individual heroism in refusing to yield her seat on the bus. Nor can it be separated from the willingness of Martin Luther King, Jr., to take responsibility for the Montgomery bus boycott; nor from the heroism of a great many other individuals.

I suspect an idea's time comes when a large enough number (a "critical mass") of individuals are willing to take personal responsibility for the whole thing. This distinguishes an idea's time coming from a social movement that may swell and then recede with no lasting impact.

Several years ago, my wife Sheila and I created a community organization aimed at blocking a massive hotel and residential complex near where we lived in Honolulu. Neither of us had organized such a group in the past, nor had we ever worked on the issues of planning and development. In other words, we had to make it up as we went along.

We announced and ran community meetings, called public officials, wrote letters to the newspapers, appeared on local radio and television shows, conducted public opinion research, polled candidates for office and published the results, recommended legislation, testified, lobbied, promised, threatened—in short, we were committed to stopping the development, nothing more or less. And we did whatever it seemed to take to accomplish that.

For about three years, stopping the development was a central activity in our lives. It was what we did. Finally the developers withdrew their request for zoning changes and gave up the project. We had won.

The point of this story is this: I can't remember any time during those three years that either Sheila or I pulled back on our commitment to stop the development. In retrospect, there were any number of opportunities when we could have settled for less. We could have been acknowledged for having "fought the good fight." We could have settled for having an impact on future development in Hawaii. We could have been satisfied to have inspired others to be more active in the future. I don't recall us ever having considered any of these options seriously. Without giving it a lot of thought at the time, we were simply committed to stopping the development, nothing more or less.

What made the project successful, however, was that Sheila and I were not alone in that degree of commitment. While the ranks of people actually doing work in support of the project sometimes swelled to a couple of hundred, there were perhaps a dozen who were as absolutely, unequivocally committed as we were. In the terms of this book, those people held themselves *personally responsible* for stopping the development. Here's a gauge of the commitment I am referring to. Had Sheila and I announced we were quitting the whole thing, one of those people would have jumped in and taken over without losing a step. As it was, their commitment showed up in a variety of ways.

One retired schoolteacher in the group felt we could make an effective point regarding the traffic congestion that would be caused by the development if we could report how many side streets and driveways fed into the main highway between the development site and the freeway, seven or eight miles away. Rather than making that as a suggestion, she got in her car and counted them.

A public health student at the university felt the most powerful argument against the development would be its impact on the already overtaxed sewage treatment plant in that area. Instead of arguing that we should concentrate on that aspect of the fight, he set about collecting and re-analyzing the data available on water quality in the area. Then he did his own water-quality testing at the site.

There are two critical qualities in actions such as these. On the one hand, they were self-inspired by people who carried out their work as though the success of the whole project depended on what they were doing. There was not the slightest feeling that they were "helping out" or "doing their part." Each acted more as though he or she were doing the whole thing. Had Sheila or I argued that the sewage issue wasn't important, I can't imagine that would have changed the public health student's actions in the slightest. He wasn't doing it to support *our* intention to stop the development, but as an expression of *his* intention. Our opinion regarding the importance of water-testing would have been mildly interesting to him at best, and he would have continued doing what he was doing.

At the same time, the people I am describing were not separate "individualists" in the negative sense of that term. In fact, they worked together closely, coordinated their actions, sought advice, listened to each other, and respected each other's participation in the project they held in common. While each individual worked as though his or her job was the most important in the whole project, that degree of commitment was not accompanied by the egotism or infighting you might expect.

All this was particularly clear in contrast to the way other people responded to our attempt to stop the development. A great many people volunteered to make limited contributions to the project. Others agreed to do so when specifically asked. It's not my intention to condemn such people by contrasting them to those I've been describing earlier. That's been the nature of *my* contribution on many other projects. And yet the contrast is a critical one. These latter people were doing *me* a favor on *my* project. It was not *their* project, even though they favored it and would benefit from it.

Here's a more poignant contrast. As I gained public attention for the work we were doing to stop the development, I began receiving telephone calls from strangers, sometimes late at night, in which I would learn about ill-advised development projects being started in other neighborhoods in Honolulu. Typically, the caller would inform me that the XYZ development company was just breaking ground on a project that had been sneaked through the government—with hints of bribery and other illegalities. Such callers clearly expected me to leap into action, grateful at having been informed of the evil about to occur. Whereas I had been holding myself personally responsible for the future quality of life in Honolulu, I found others willing to hold me responsible, also.

If you think about it, this is the way we normally treat people who voluntarily act in the public interest. Once someone has stepped forward, the rest of us tend to pull back. We are free to criticize the way the job is getting done and even blame the "leader" for any failures, but we do not feel obliged to take over. Not satisfied with the state of automobile safety? It's more likely that you'll blame Ralph Nader than that you'll take the issue on yourself. If Nader weren't so abrasive, if only he had more of a sense of humor, maybe if he were willing to compromise now and again, there would probably be more progress. Right?

An idea's time does not come, I suggest, when a mass of people are willing to let someone else be responsible. An idea's time comes when a critical mass of individuals are willing to hold themselves personally responsible and act in a manner appropriate to that responsibility. Sometimes all those individuals will act in concert with one another, coordinating their actions, respecting and supporting each other. Sometimes the situation is very different.

Black civil rights did not become an idea whose time had come in America because all those active in the movement agreed. Fortunately, the movement did not depend on Martin Luther King, Jr., and Malcolm X agreeing on what needed to be done. Neither one made his commitment dependent on that of the other. Progress was made because each of these men—

and a great many other men and women—were willing to be totally responsible, no matter what anyone else did. When people start quarreling about *how* to accomplish something, we tend to lose sight of the fact that they are no longer debating *whether.*

Like a Hologram

It seems to me that the relationship between individual responsibility and an idea's time coming is somewhat holographic. A hologram is a three-dimensional projection created through a special application of laser technology. You can walk around a holographic projection and see the front and the back of the image being created. In the movie *Star Wars* the appeal R2D2 carried from Princess Leia to Obi-Wan Kenobi was in the form of a hologram.

A peculiar quality of holography is that if you cut up a holographic film into tiny pieces, each of those pieces contains and can project the entire image! Contrast this with a normal photograph you might take of your Aunt Lizzie. Cut the negative into little pieces, and each piece will only reproduce some part of Lizzie's anatomy. Had you taken a hologram, however, any piece would give you the whole lady: the larger the piece, the brighter the projection.

I suspect that one person acting on the basis of total personal responsibility can cause an idea's time to come, eventually. With several individuals so inclined, that idea's time will come much faster. The more people taking total responsibility, the faster its time will come.

Imagine, for a moment, that every man, woman, and child on this planet—all 4.6 billion of us—were to take personal responsibility for, say, ending world hunger. Take a minute to imagine that you had made such a commitment, that your life was now dedicated to ending hunger. Imagine how you would just naturally act in various situations. Now imagine every man, woman, and child on the planet acting on such a commitment. Imagine that all 4.6 billion of us had made the ending of hunger our number one personal commitment. How long would hunger last? A day? Given the worst possible logistical problems, maybe a week.

Clearly I am not talking about more individuals being responsible for more *parts* of the whole. I am talking about each being totally responsible for the whole thing. That's the kind of heroism called for in the world today. In the next chapter, we'll see what that looks like in practice.

6. ENDING HUNGER

Life, misfortunes, isolation, abandonment, poverty are
battlefields which have their heroes; obscure heroes,
sometimes greater than the illustrious heroes.

—Victor Hugo

While it's not altogether clear what it takes to cause an idea's time to come, finding out is sufficiently important for us to look further into the matter. Let's examine a major social problem that may shed some light on the the role of individuals and organizations in bringing about a profound social change. We'll examine the issue of world hunger.[1] I want to begin by quoting at length from a rather unusual letter I received the other day.

Dear Earl and Sheila:

We did it! At 8 A.M., a week ago Sunday (February 5), I went to the starting line of the Oakland marathon with your pledge of $100.00 plus other pledges and matching funds totalling $41,000, a thousand dollars over our goal!

Unfortunately, however, this marked the completion of only the *first* step. Next was the marathon itself. The week before I injured a muscle in my left calf so badly I had to take a taxi home from the Golden Gate Bridge. I was hoping a week with no running would allow it to heal sufficiently to take me 26.2 miles.

Not so . . . after the first two miles my leg was hurting so badly I had to start walking. My running partner—Jim Ray (58 years old!) offered to run it on my behalf. I agreed and told him I'd walk the half-marathon and meet him at the finish (I figured 8–10 hours to walk the whole marathon, which I did not want to do).

He took off—I kept walking. This got boring pretty fast. So I found a running pace (slow) and a posture (body straight upright, not leaning forward) that didn't hurt too badly, and I started running again. I was sure my muscle, even under these running conditions, wouldn't last too long—so I asked a race official to take my number on up to Jim so he could carry it with him, figuring at the minimum my *number* should complete the course even if I didn't.

Then I started writing the completion letter to you in my head:

"Dear Earl and Sheila, Well, we raised $41,000 but I didn't quite do the whole marathon . . . I had this bad muscle, you see, and . . ."

As much as I rewrote it, a certain quality of inspiration was somehow lacking. Before I knew it, I had missed the half-marathon turn-off and was at the 13-mile point for the *full* marathon. Plus, the race official brought my number back because he couldn't find Jim! The only way out was to complete the entire course!

Which I did—happily, albeit painfully. Other than at the beginning, I never had to walk—the letter I wrote during the second half was far better than the first. The whole thing took 4 hours and 20 minutes (another personal record—for the longest time!), with dozens of Hunger Project volunteers, World Runners and friends cheering me at the finish as though I had just broken a world record.

Gordon Starr is one of the heroes who will end world hunger, and his story can shed light on what it takes to cause an idea's time to come. Several years ago, Gordon committed himself to run a marathon every year until hunger is ended on the planet, asking people to pledge money to that end every time he runs. He says of the 1984 Oakland experience:

> Something more than just running and contributing money happened this year. There was an excitement, a partnership, an involvement expressed that made me certain the condition of starvation doesn't stand a chance to persist beyond the end of the century. Not with people like this group going for its throat.

People Are Starving

While it is impossible to calculate such things precisely, it is generally estimated that some 13 to 18 million people die as a consequence of starvation worldwide each year. Strictly speaking, almost no one dies of hunger per se; instead, people who are malnourished (lacking specific nutrients) or chronically undernourished (lacking nutrients generally) die of diseases and other conditions that you and I recover from. We catch the measles and recover; others die. The same goes for colds, the flu, diarrhea, and any number of other maladies. What merely represents discomfort for you and me spells death for the hungry.

It's difficult to communicate the magnitude of world hunger. It's simply too horrible for most people to confront. Deaths due to hunger average out to over forty thousand a day! Recall the last time you saw a newspaper headline that proclaimed TWO HUNDRED KILLED IN AIRLINE CRASH in two-inch letters, or 2,000 FEARED DEAD IN EARTHQUAKE. Anything that kills hundreds of people, certainly anything that kills thousands, is worth stopping the presses for. And yet over forty thousand die of hunger every day. That works out to about twenty-eight every minute of every day throughout the year, and three-fourths of them are children.

Today, we are horrified to recall (or to first learn) that the nuclear bomb dropped on Hiroshima in 1945 killed 125,000 people. And yet, hunger kills that many people every three days —all through the year, every year. In 1976, an earthquake in China—the worst in modern history—killed 242,000 people. That many people die of hunger every six days.

Hunger simply dwarfs the other causes of death that concern us. Wars can't compare. Highway deaths are trivial in comparison with hunger. Murders are a drop in the bucket.

Given the magnitude of the insult that hunger is to the human race, why do we let it persist? Here's the beginning of an answer.

One night in 1976, I happened to watch a TV documentary on world hunger with Aaron, who was seven at the time. It was pretty grim and depressing, filled with skin-and-bones children. I'm not sure why we started watching it, but we both got hooked on it. The more we watched it, the more moved both of us became. When the program ended, both of us just sat quietly for awhile. Then Aaron came to me and solemnly announced, "Daddy, I'd like to skip dinner tonight and have you send my food to those children who don't have anything to eat."

Aaron's reaction to the program was probably typical of hundreds, even thousands of children that night. My reaction to him was probably equally typical of parents. I told him his concern was really beautiful and that I was proud of him. I told him his compassion for others showed what a good person he was. Then, I began an unconscious process of "cooling out" my son. I pointed out to him that the problem was more complicated than he thought. I told him it wouldn't work for me to send his food through the mail—"I wouldn't know where to send it, and it wouldn't keep anyway"—and I said it was more important for him to eat his dinner, grow up strong, and *then* perhaps he would be able to do something about the problem of starving children.

In the space of a few minutes, I had effectively convinced Aaron that the problem of world hunger was too big and too complicated for him to handle. In the process, I added weight to the view that he couldn't really make a difference in the world. It's still painful for me to think back on that night, since it was such a perfect example of the process that has kept starvation existing in the world for as long as we know. It's the same process that dampens heroism in the world more generally.

Enter The Hunger Project

My next contact with world hunger came in March 1977, when I went to San Francisco for a meeting of the est Advisory Board. The est training is a program of personal transformation created in 1971 by Werner Erhard, and the Advisory Board was a group of some forty or fifty people from various walks of life, who had taken the est training and who met two or three times a year to advise Erhard on what est should be doing in the world.

At the March 1977 meeting, Erhard announced that he had been researching the problem of world hunger for several years and was now ready to make a personal commitment to bringing it to an end. Although he was still not clear as to what it would take to end hunger, he was committing himself to doing whatever that might be. To add reality to his commitment, he announced that he was creating an organization, called The Hunger Project, in collaboration with composer-singer John Denver (an Advisory Board member) and Dr. Robert Fuller, former president of Oberlin College and then director of The est Foundation.

My own first reaction to the announcement was negative. As a sociologist and as someone who had been deeply involved in the issue of overpopulation, I felt certain that any attempt to end hunger would result in disaster. It would surely result in even greater overpopulation, producing even greater hunger in the long run. The commitment to end hunger seemed naïve and ill-advised. I was concerned that some people I loved and respected were about to look very stupid. And I'm sure I was worried that I'd look stupid by association.

At the outset, Erhard laid out what he regarded as the four major principles that needed to guide the end of hunger. First, The Hunger Project was to be grounded in individual and personal responsibility. Ending hunger could not be held as the task of government or of large corporations. It needed to flow naturally from how individuals personally felt about their planet.

> If you have to keep people fired up, this project is a joke.
> If this project isn't natural to your Self, this project is a fraud.

Second, Erhard spoke of the project as an "alignment of wholes, not a sum of parts." By this, he meant that hunger could not be ended by a mass of individuals, each of whom would agree to do his or her part. Everyone involved in the project needed to be operating on the basis of a total, personal commitment to getting the job done. The Hunger Project, as a whole, would be the coming together of similarly committed individuals. At the same time, ironically, no one would be able to take credit for ending hunger. The desire to take credit, whether it appeared among individuals in The Hunger Project or in its relationship with other anti-hunger organizations, would be an obstacle to getting the job done.

Third, The Hunger Project was to focus more on *context* than on *content.* In Erhard's own research into world hunger, he had concluded that we already possessed everything we needed to know about the mechanics of ending hunger. We didn't need new strains of rice or new methods for storing or distributing food. Advances in these domains would be welcomed, of course, but they would not be sufficient to end world hunger any more than past developments had done so.

Erhard noted that there were already thousands of committed individuals working through numerous organizations in the trenches of the war on hunger. Whenever famines or similar disasters appeared on the planet, organizations such as Oxfam, Catholic Relief Services, the American Friends Service Committee, UNICEF, CARE, and many others sprang into action. Organizations like Save the Children sought to provide continuing assistance to hungry children everywhere. Others, like Bread for the World, engaged in active lobbying efforts to get legislation and other government action to relieve the problem of hunger. The people involved in these organizations knew what was needed, worked heroically, and made profound contributions to people around the world. And yet, without broad public support, they were fighting a holding action.

What was missing, Erhard concluded, was a global context of commitment to use what tools we had and actually end hunger. For my part, I recalled growing up during World War II and remembered how everyone you met every day was deeply and personally concerned about the war and how it was going. Then I recalled the Vietnam era, when *Newsweek* had a regular weekly section on the war. I began to imagine what it would be like if *Newsweek* had a weekly section addressing world hunger. What would it be like if everyone you met was eager for news on how we were doing?

At about the same time The Hunger Project was being organized, the National Academy of Sciences issued a report on their two-year, definitive examination of world hunger, involving the efforts of some fifteen hundred individuals and organizations. Their ultimate conclusion was that the world now possessed everything it would take to end world hunger. All that was lacking, they added, was the "political will" to get it done.

The final generating principle of The Hunger Project was that of *transformation*. Erhard suggested that consciously and deliberately ending world hunger would both require and produce a transformation in the way human beings occupied their planet. If we were successful in joining together to defeat one of the Four Horsemen of the Apocalypse, successful in ending the misery of a billion human beings, we would never be the same again. As a human race, we could not end hunger and then return to being the hapless victims of "forces beyond our control." We could hardly hold that the problems of poverty, injustice, war, and the like were too big to be handled.

By the end of the meeting, I had committed myself, personally and professionally, to the end of world hunger. The changes I went through in my own mind with regard to the problem of world hunger had a powerful impact on my sociological understanding of such problems and certainly clarified my appreciation of the role to be played by individuals in solving major social problems.

Can Hunger Really Be Ended?

In the most literal sense, there will never be a time after which no human being will ever die for lack of food. There will always be people who get lost in the desert and starve. There will always be isolated individuals and groups who, unknown to the rest of us, are dying for lack of food. Moreover, there will probably always be famine situations, known to us at the time, in which people will starve before assistance arrives.

None of the above comments, however, invalidates the commitment to an *end* of hunger on the planet. Nor does it mean that we can only hope to make hunger *less* of a problem. None of those comments needs deny the vision of an end to hunger as "an idea whose time has come." Here's why that's so.

Today, we live in a global condition in which 13 to 18 million human beings die as a consequence of hunger every year. It is the *condition* in which we live our lives, just as we live in a condition of gravity. Everything we do occurs within and is a function of that condition. Our experience of who we are is "conditioned" by the fact that over forty thousand of us die of hunger every day. Those deaths are not exceptions to some rule;

they are part of it. The death by hunger of twenty-eight people a minute is part of the *routine* of life on our planet at the present time.

Consider this analogy. Many of the world's cities exist today in a condition of air pollution. Some days, the air is fairly clear; other days it is terrible; but every day is lived in a condition of air pollution.

Now suppose that all the world's cities were to eliminate the condition of air pollution. Imagine that we did everything it took for all the ecological experts to agree that air pollution had been eliminated. That would not mean there would never be any air pollution. Forest fires and volcanic eruptions would, from time to time, pollute the air. Chemical plants would explode now and then, causing air pollution. All such events would be an exception to the condition of "no pollution," rather than a part of a routine condition of pollution. Those exceptions would be worthy of note in the world's newpaper headlines.

Now, consider the analogy of airplane crashes. Although there is some statistical average for the number of people who die in airplane accidents each year, we do not live in a condition of airplane accidents. Whenever an airplane crashes, we regard that as a tragic exception, not the rule. Those responsible for air safety undertake an immediate search for answers and actions. When the cause of the accident is discovered, steps are taken to insure that it won't happen again: airplanes are redesigned, air traffic control procedures are revised, pilot licensing is tightened up. All this occurs because we live in a condition of no accidents.

When the condition of world hunger has been eliminated on the planet, people will undoubtedly die for lack of food from time to time, but their deaths will not be regarded as routine. They will be held as tragedies. They will be tragically worthy of newspaper headlines and, more important, they will be taken as a signal for concerted efforts to insure that they are not repeated. People will be shocked. They will ask, "How could that have happened?" and demand to know what can and is being done to insure that it never happens again.

It is worth noting that the condition of no accidents has made air travel safer and safer. Every airplane crash, in fact, contributes to air safety. In a condition of no hunger, every death by hunger makes future deaths less likely.

The shift from a condition of hunger-as-usual to one of no hunger is an example of what is often called *social transformation.* It is something far more profound than simple change, like the rise and fall of interest rates or hemlines. Transformation represents a discontinuity in the flow of things. It is as though the line fluctuating up and down on the two-dimensional graph abruptly disappears and reappears on a different graph, a four-dimensional one in fact.

Here's a different example of what I mean by transformation in this sense. Throughout the history of slavery in America, a body of legislation and of court decisions kept changing the nature of black-white relations, sometimes making slavery more severe, sometimes more lenient. The Emancipation Proclamation, which abolished slavery altogether, however, represented transformation rather than mere change.

Often, great social transformations come in the form of "an idea whose time has come." I want to spend the rest of this chapter by looking at what it will take to bring about the end of world hunger as an idea whose time has come. What will it take to bring about a global transformation from a condition of hunger-as-usual to one of no hunger?

The Structure of Hunger's Persistence

Over the course of the past seven years, I have talked about world hunger to a very wide range of groups—literally from kindergarten classes to senior citizen clubs. The nature of those interactions has revealed a great deal about the social-psychological structure of the *persistence* of world hunger. I stress the "persistence" of hunger, since hunger itself needs little or no explanation: people die as a consequence of hunger because they don't have enough to eat. No mystery there. The question, rather, is why we allow the condition of world hunger to persist.

Over the course of the past seven years, I suspect I have heard every explanation there is for the persistence of hunger—and have begun to grasp the structure that holds all those explanations together. At the top of the structure, many people say they are unaware that hunger is a major problem in the world today. They may recall Biblical reports of famines in the distant past and even remember something about people being hungry in Europe after World War II.

Interestingly, I've never had anyone argue with the assertion that hunger is a massive problem in the world. Even those who say they didn't know hunger was still a problem do not react to the news with disbelief. Rather, they act as though they suspected it was true and didn't want to know for sure.

Once people acknowledge that hunger is a major problem, they begin offering explanations for its persistence. The first explanation usually is that there simply isn't enough food for everyone. Here's where people put the blame on overpopulation, as I had done initially. Many people have some vague recollection of Malthus saying that food production increased arithmetically while population grew geometrically. Moreover, people point out, India is a good example of a greatly overpopulated country and one that has a big problem of hunger. In fact, the fabled large welfare families in this country would seem to fit into that pattern.

As compelling as this explanation is, it conflicts with the hard, cold facts. This has been pointed out in numerous ways. For example, during the past quarter-century, world food production has been increasing faster than population growth. More to the point, the world's current production of grain alone equals three thousand calories' worth per person per day worldwide—about the number of calories consumed daily by Americans at the present time. Remember, this is just the grain we produce. It doesn't take account of other foodstuffs—vegetables, fruit, fish, etc.—and it ignores the fact that many American farmers are actually being paid to hold back on what they produce.

No matter how you cut it, the persistence of hunger on the planet cannot be explained as a function of scarcity. It's been estimated that we produce enough food right now to feed 7 billion people. And yet, of the world's 4.6 billion inhabitants, about a billion go to bed hungry every night. So how can that be?

Once people have acknowledged that scarcity is not the cause of hunger's persistence, they have other explanations. (It's ironic that everyone seems to know why hunger persists. Almost nobody says, "People are starving? How come?") Most of the explanations offered at this point are logistical (e.g., too difficult to get food where the people are), economic (e.g., people need money with which to grow or buy food), political (e.g., corrupt officials divert the food), ideological (e.g., capitalism is the problem), and so forth. These kinds of explanations are different from the earlier ones.

There's often some truth in explanations like these. Food distribution *is* often difficult. The problem of hunger *is* inextricable from the economic systems within which it appears. Corrupt officials *do* sometimes steal the food intended for the poor. Yet none of these kinds of reasons is a sufficient explanation for the persistence of hunger in the world. Perhaps the most powerful argument against this explanation is the variety of conditions under which nations have ended hunger in the past. To see this, we need to take a moment to consider how we would know if hunger had been ended in a country.

For the experts in this field, the best indication of whether hunger is a national problem is found in that nation's *infant mortality rate* (IMR): the number of children per thousand who die during their first year, as I've already discussed in chapter 1. Now obviously children die of many causes, and even in the best case—Sweden—seven out of every thousand children die before reaching their first birthdays. Some IMRs are *much* higher, however. Some African countries, as we saw earlier, have infant mortality rates in excess of two hundred: more than one out of every five children dies in its first year.

Very high infant mortality rates are recognized by the experts as a good indication that hunger is a basic problem for that society. The rule of thumb—adopted by UNICEF, the World Health Organization, and many other researchers and organizations—is that an IMR of fifty or more indicates that hunger is a basic problem for a country. There are few nations with IMRs in the vicinity of fifty, by the way: most are either substantially below it or substantially above it, making a pretty clear distinction between the haves and the have-nots.

During this century, some fifty-three nations with populations of a million or more have reduced their infant mortality rates from above fifty to below it, thus apparently ending hunger as a basic problem for their people. Thirty-five have done so since World War II. Of particular relevance to our present discussion, those nations have ended hunger in a wide variety of ways. Some, like South Korea, have done so by emphasizing agriculture, while agriculture has played little or no part in the achievement in countries like Hong Kong, for example. Communist countries, like the USSR, have ended hunger; so have liberal democracies like Costa Rica and right-wing dictatorships like Chile. In Japan, the national government played a central role in ending hunger; in Spain, by contrast, the government was not very involved. In Taiwan, the family farm was the key to ending hunger; in the People's Republic of China, collective agriculture produced the same result. Some countries have required massive foreign aid, others have ended hunger without it. Some of the OPEC nations have ended hunger as a consequence of becoming very rich, while other countries—Sri Lanka is an example—have ended hunger even while remaining very poor as a nation.

Ultimately, it comes down to this. Whatever reason may be given for the persistence of hunger in the world, there is some country that has solved the problem of hunger in spite of that reason. We need to look elsewhere for the explanation for the persistence of hunger.

Growing Up and Becoming "Realistic"

One of the true joys in my life during the past seven years has involved talking to young children about hunger. That doesn't seem like a very joyous undertaking, I know, but it has provided me with some of the most powerfully moving moments of my life.

I'll always remember the first time I was asked to meet with a kindergarten class in Honolulu shortly after The Hunger Project was created. A friend who operated a large preschool had decided it was important to let the children in her school know about the problem of world hunger, as long as it was handled in a way that would support and empower the children rather than simply making them feel bad. She asked me to meet with one of her kindergarten classes.

I can still remember standing on the concrete walkway outside the second-story classroom door, waiting to go in, still not sure how to talk to really young kids about something as depressing as world hunger. As I look back on it now, I can see that my main problem was that *I* didn't really think there was much a kindergarten child could do about world hunger.

When the time came, however, the door to the classroom opened, and I had no choice. My friend invited me into the room and announced, "All right boys and girls. This is Mr. Babbie, and he's going to talk with us about something I know you will want to know about." With that, I was treated to a series of shocks.

First, I had totally forgotten how small kindergarten children were. The classroom consisted of about four fairly large tables with about eight children sitting at each. But the tables seemed to be no more than perhaps a foot off the floor, and the children's heads seemed to reach about a foot and a half at most. I was seized by a real concern that I would step on someone or trip and fall.

Second, I had not been prepared for the children's openness and genuine love for this stranger who had stumbled into their midst. When I was introduced, they all clapped their hands and cheered. Then they settled back in a clearly excited anticipation. I was on.

In that first encounter with kindergarten children, I discovered that I am naturally more of a Mister Rogers than a Captain Kangaroo. I quickly found it possible to say things like "Hi, boys and girls" without feeling foolish or trite, and found myself naturally emphasizing all the appropriate emotions as I talked to them. "How would you like to play a game?" I asked brightly, imagining a cartoon drawing of a light bulb going on over my head. "Yay!" they all shouted in unison, squirming around in their shrunken seats and glancing back and forth among themselves in excited anticipation. And so we began our journey off to confront world hunger.

"I want you to imagine what you would do if you sat down at the table to color, and you found the table covered with books," I started. "What would you do?" About half the children shouted some version of "Move the books." "That's right!" I replied, and we all cheered.

"Now suppose you wanted to dance around the floor, and the chairs were in your way. What would you do?" I asked. "Move them!" everyone shouted, and we all cheered again. I could see we were on a roll.

"What if you came into the classroom and found that all the books had fallen off the bookshelf. What would you do?" "Put them back," came the chorus. "Suppose this raincoat fell off the hook." I stepped quickly to a wall covered with raincoats on hooks (about a foot off the floor). A small Japanese boy shouted, "I'd hang it up!" And he looked proudly around the room as everyone cheered.

At that point, I launched into a more professorial talk about how, when we don't like the way we find things, we just fix them. We shifted from the classroom to some other real life situations. "Suppose you were in the Ala Moana shopping center with your mom or your dad, and you found a little boy who was crying because he couldn't find his parents. What would you do?" The children had no problem finding solutions. "I'd tell my mother." "I'd take him to the police." "I'd hold his hand and say 'Don't worry. We'll find your parents.' " I posed several problems to the children, and they quickly found solutions to them all. Where appropriate, they showed genuine compassion for the people who had the problem, and they always showed a determination to set things right.

Getting more serious, I asked if they had ever been hungry. "Can you remember a time when you were waiting for dinner to be ready, and you were kind of a pest, asking 'When do we eat?' over and over again. Or did you ever come home from school so hungry that you had a snack before dinner?" Everybody could remember such times.

"Well, there are some children in the world that are very, very hungry all day, every day. And their parents are so poor, they don't have anything to give the children to eat. Many of those children are so hungry, they'll die if something isn't done right away." I'd finally reached the point of my being in the classroom that day. The response was far different from anything I'd imagined, standing outside the door waiting to go inside.

The children in the class took the plight of the hungry children very seriously. There was no joking or kidding around. Nobody acted silly during that part of the day's discussion. They exhibited varying degrees of concern, distress, alarm, even sorrow. And yet, there was no evidence of them being beaten down or subdued by the tragic news. Their reactions were far different from those of any adults I had discussed hunger with.

Whereas the news of world hunger often has a deadening effect on adults, it made the kindergarten children *more alive*. They wanted to *do something*—just as Aaron had that night two years before. For many of them, the most obvious thing to do was to give up their lunches, and several offered to turn them over to me so the children wouldn't starve. Some offered to bring more food from home. Others said they would tell their parents about the problem so they could do something. "I'll tell my father. He can fix things like that." As a bottom line, they were simply unwilling to have children starve, and they wanted to do something about it right away.

As I reviewed my encounter with that kindergarten class, I initially decided that I had been really clever about the way I led up to the problem of hunger, dealing with simple examples of taking action when we don't like the way we find things. As it turns out, I gave myself too much credit in the matter.

Any time I have discussed world hunger with young children since then, they have always wanted to *do something* right away, no matter how I have led up to it. I've become aware that there's no need for me to plant the idea of making a difference; it's already there and simply obvious to anyone under six years of age.

Since I have spoken about hunger to every age group from kindergarten to senior citizens, I have had the unusual opportunity to observe an approximation of the growing-up process that individuals go through. It's been an enlightening and also a sobering experience.

Up to about junior high school, the young people I've met with simply leap into action. The main difference between kindergarten and, say, seventh grade, is that as children get older, their actions become more potent. Whereas a five-year-old is likely to want to send his or her sandwich to Somalia, older children may decide they can accomplish more by raising money for relief efforts, writing letters to public officials, and so forth.

At one point I was asked to meet with a seventh grade class in Nanakuli, a poor, rural, and predominantly Hawaiian community on the west end of Oahu, about forty-five minutes drive from downtown Honolulu. Although this was my first time inside a Nanakuli classroom, I came equipped with a full set of stereotypes. I'd been warned that the students in Nanakuli were not very academically inclined and that there was a lot of violence in the classroom. Friends joked about how I should leave my wallet at home, take a spare set of tires for the car, et cetera. I laughed at the jokes, but I made a point of parking my car as near the administration building as possible, and I transferred some money from my wallet to my shirt pocket—just in case.

I got to the classroom without any incident but, once I was there, my concerns began to grow. The students came into the classroom with a fair amount of shoving and horseplay. Moreover, the boys were much bigger than typical seventh graders. The stereotype about Hawaiians being bigger than average is well-grounded in fact.

As soon as I began talking about the problem of world hunger, however, the classroom seemed totally transformed. At the least, my experience of it was transformed. The horsing around ceased, students stopped talking to one another and were clearly taking in every word I said. They asked questions. They wanted to understand the details of hunger in the world.

It was as though understanding about world hunger was somehow vital to their own well-being. Eventually, I saw that hunger *was* very real in their lives. Although none of them was actually starving, they were poor enough to have known times when food was scarce, even in tropical Hawaii. This was no theoretical discussion for them. "Eh, I know two old people near my house that sometimes don't have nothing to eat. Last week, my Auntie took them some mango and banana. We should take some food to them."

By the time I left the classroom, the students had organized themselves to collect canned goods and to locate hungry people in their neighborhood.

In the best of all worlds, people would continue becoming more effective in such matters while maintaining their commitment to doing something. In fact, something peculiar seems to occur at around the beginning of high school. If you were to speak to a freshman class in high school about the problem of world hunger, you would probably find most of the students interested in and concerned about what you had to say. A few of the students, however, would probably appear to be almost unconscious. Even though they would have their eyes open and might even be looking in your general direction, you would have the distinct impression that they were not really alive. Images from *The Night of the Living Dead* might run through your head.

If you spoke to sophomore, junior, and senior classes, you would probably find the proportion of zombies increasing as the students got older. I'm reluctant to talk this way, since I know it will seem as though I want to belittle the students. That's definitely not my purpose, and yet I know of no more accurate description of the glazed-over, "nobody home" look that seems to become more prevalent as young people move through high school. When you speak to a group of students about the fact that 13 to 18 million people die of hunger each year, they don't seem surprised, they don't seem to feel bad about it, they're not happy: ultimately, nothing you say seems to register at all. It's an eerie experience.

Although I cannot say so with any certainty, I suspect the phenomenon I've been describing is the result of young people being told they are not capable of making a difference, even being ridiculed for their "naïve" concerns and intentions to save the world. I was in high school at the time of the Montgomery bus boycott. Living in a small town in New Hampshire, I had hardly ever seen a black person, and I had no idea about conditions in the South. When I first learned that blacks had to sit in the back of the bus, I thought that was stupid. Why on earth should they have to sit in the back of the bus? Let 'em sit anywhere they wanted. When I began learning that blacks were being brutalized because of their refusal to abide by the rules of segregation, I was outraged.

I remember going to my teachers and my parents with the demand and expectation that something be done about segregation in the South. It was then I learned that "things were more complicated than I knew." It turned out that I didn't know anything at all about the history of race relations in the South. I hadn't given much thought to both blacks and whites growing up, being taught a particular way of behaving toward one another. I certainly didn't know anything about the economics of race relations, nor of the political dimension. And there I was, naïvely demanding that everything be turned on its head. Ultimately, I got very quiet about the whole thing. I resolved to learn more about the world before I spouted off about things I didn't really understand.

I suspect that's the same kind of quiet I confronted in talking to high school students about world hunger. It seems to me as though they had "learned their place" in the scheme of things —that they shouldn't get involved in things they didn't understand or commit themselves to "naïve causes" in which they couldn't really make a difference.

Speaking to somewhat older people has been a little different but not really better. On the whole, college students have been no more committed to making a difference than the high school students I've been describing, but they are noisier about it. While we might conclude that high school students are quietly devastated by the discovery that they don't make a difference, college students are able to explain why they don't make a difference.

Speaking to college students about world hunger is to invite lengthy discussions about how the world works, how complicated it is, and why things can't be changed. None of this is to deny past periods of radicalism among college students—students are less radical today than in the sixties and seventies— or to deny the impact students have, in fact, had on national and world events. We'd probably be one-fourth of the way to a Hundred Years War in Vietnam except for the role of the nation's college students in opposing it. The cause of human rights, with its many faces, has depended heavily on students.

There exists a real irony in the midst of campus activism. Side by side with powerful movements of social reform can be found a massive pall of "it can't be done" and "nothing matters." Nor am I describing two different sets of students. Often those who have committed their lives to social reform are convinced that they will ultimately fail. According to a left-wing point of view, the entrenched forces of the military-industrial complex will ultimately crush all who get in their way. All one can hope to do is make a noble gesture, perhaps a mighty one, but ultimately it will not change things.

As I have spoken to older groups about world hunger, I've heard many of the same explanations college students give, reinforced by the fact that older people have a longer history of not feeling they make a difference. I ran smack into this in my very first presentation on world hunger in Honolulu.

Shortly after I returned to Honolulu from the est Advisory Board meeting, my mother invited me to speak to her Senior Citizens Club. She was the program chairman and was delighted to have an excuse to show off her son. So we arranged for me to come to the club one noon to tell them about world hunger, The Hunger Project, and what the club members could do to end starvation in the world.

My main presentation went very well. I'd been introduced and presented with a lei. I told them the main facts about hunger, emphasizing that it could be ended. I suggested various things they might do to fight hunger, and I told them about a Hunger Project event that was coming soon, with a six-dollar admission fee.

One of the ladies in the club asked a question. "How can I be sure this is real?"

"Excuse me?"

"How can I be sure that this really is what you say it is? I sent money to Boys' Town for years. I sent five dollars every month, even when it was really hard for me to scrape together the money. Any time I would think 'Maybe I won't send it this month,' I'd think about those poor orphans who needed it more than me."

She swallowed and continued her story. "Then one day I read in the paper that Boys' Town had millions of dollars in the bank." Her eyes scanned the room. "I felt stupid for scraping together five dollars every month when they had more money than I will ever see."

Now her eyes finally came to rest on me. "I feel really bad about the people who are starving, and I want to help, but how can I be sure this isn't something else I'll feel stupid about later?"

It was one of those situations you appreciate in retrospect, an opportunity for learning—not unlike learning to swim by falling into the ocean. There I stood, in front of my mother and her friends, asked a powerful question I couldn't answer.

While the gears of my mind whirred around and around in search of an answer, I heard myself answering. "You *can't* be sure, really. If you pay six dollars to come to the presentation I mentioned, or if you give money to some other organization to fight hunger, there's no way you can be absolutely certain you won't feel conned later on. I'm afraid that's an unavoidable risk of trying to make a difference. Ultimately, I guess, you have to weigh how much you want to end hunger against how much you don't want to look stupid."

Instead of me answering her question, it was as though someone else were answering *mine*. All this time, I had been worried about the possibility of looking stupid because of my participation in The Hunger Project. Now I saw that I very well might look stupid. That was the price of trying to make a difference in the world. Oh. Somehow, knowing that was very liberating for me.

The differences I've observed in speaking about hunger to a spectrum of age groups are similar to the process of growing up I've experienced personally, and I suspect the same may be true for you as well. As a young child and continuing up to high school, I was unabashedly committed to making the world better. When I saw things that just weren't the way they were supposed to be, I tended to leap into action. Then, somewhere during high school and college, I underwent a subtle shift in the way I approached life. I learned that I was powerless to do anything about the way things were. So, I pretty much gave up trying. My own experience with The Hunger Project and with my study of heroism more generally has recreated in me the possibility of making a difference. The willingness to step out and take a chance has been rekindled as well.

My own experience in this regard has not been unique. During the past few years, the issue of world hunger—both within The Hunger Project and outside it—has sparked true heroism in individuals again and again. The total, personal commitment which seems needed to cause an idea's time to come is alive and growing in the war against hunger, and it is my privilege to report some examples of that in concluding this chapter.

Individuals in Action

Joan Holmes

Joan Holmes is an excellent first example of an individual taking responsibility for world hunger. When Erhard announced his commitment to ending hunger, Holmes gave up a successful career as a school psychologist and volunteered to be responsible for bringing the project into existence as interim manager.

While Hunger Project founders Erhard, Denver, and Fuller initially looked for a nationally prominent person to take the position of executive director, things turned out rather differently. Within a few months, it became clear to them that Joan Holmes was exactly the person for the job. She had demonstrated repeatedly her fundamental grasp of the generating principles of The Hunger Project and what it would take to put them into action.

For Holmes's part, becoming executive director of The Hunger Project meant creating a twenty-year, personal commitment to the end of hunger. It's worth noting that nothing in her previous career pointed logically toward her new job. Nor was there any guarantee that her decision would prove a wise one. No one expected Holmes to take on the end of hunger. The world was not clamoring for The Hunger Project. In short, nothing reasonable pointed toward the dramatic shift in her life. Joan Holmes became personally responsible for the end of world hunger in the same way Martin Luther King, Jr., became responsible for civil rights and Ralph Nader became responsible for consumers' rights: *because she said so.*

By the fall of 1983, Joan Holmes had become successful by any measure. The Hunger Project had become respected throughout the hunger-response community. With 2.6 million individuals having enrolled themselves in the project, and in the cause of the end of world hunger, The Hunger Project was the largest private voluntary organization in the world. Holmes was now accustomed to meeting with leading scientists and heads of state around the world. From an ordinary human point of view, Joan Holmes had taken a chance but made good on it. Now, she could sit back and enjoy the life of a prestigious international leader.

By fall 1983, however, Joan Holmes had concluded that the time had come for The Hunger Project to move into the trenches and challenge hunger face-to-face. Having developed a powerful and well-trained staff in San Francisco, Holmes now created a three-person executive body to run the San Francisco office, and she moved to Bombay to establish The Hunger Project in India.

It is estimated that one-third of all the world's hungry people live in India. The second most populous country in the world, India is divided by language, religion, ethnicity, politics, class, and caste. More recovery and development programs have failed in India than in any other country. In short, all the circumstances argue against The Hunger Project having any impact in India.

In Holmes's view, her mission is not to "take The Hunger Project to India" but to provide an opportunity for it to arise among the Indian people. Rather than pity, she brings with her a respect for the ability of individual Indians to take on the problem of hunger and end it, and she is personally committed to forming a partnership with them in that. So all the circumstances are against the success of the partnership? Holmes replies: "An individual's word is more powerful than circumstances."

Monique Grodzki

In 1979, Monique Grodzki was a nine-year-old growing up in suburban New York when she happened to see a television documentary on the plight of Cambodian refugees.[2] While moved by the tragedy of it all, Monique was more powerfully struck by the people's undaunted spirit. "I found it amazing that they were still singing and had the hope and strength to go on. After I saw that, I actually cried. I really had to do something about it."

Monique was also moved by the discovery that children suffer most from hunger and from war. In her view, children should have a say about wars, about government: "They should have a say about things in general, about things that affect them." Monique resolved to give children a say in establishing the priorities of the world. "We're putting millions and billions of dollars into nuclear armaments. Wouldn't it be better to have a 'stop world hunger' race than a nuclear armament race?"

The Children's Peace Committee was the result of Monique's resolve: its purpose to "help abolish world hunger and promote world peace." By 1982, a growing membership of two hundred children aged ten to thirteen were actively engaged in a variety of activities. They've addressed the general public at the Dag Hammarskjold Plaza of the United Nations, circulated petitions, collected money and sent it to organizations fighting hunger in the field. Looking closer to home, they raised money to buy bullet-proof vests for police officers in New York, and contributed to the family of an officer killed in the line of duty. More important than the specific activities of Monique and her friends is the simple fact of their willingness to take responsibility for something much bigger than anyone would expect a child to comprehend. If nothing else, it makes it that much harder for adults to feel too small to make a difference.

Leonard Solomon
Harold Solomon

Leonard Solomon, president of Budget Rent-A-Car in Miami, found that one way to bring public attention to the problem of world hunger was to put Hunger Project bumper stickers on all the Budget cars in Southern Florida and New Orleans. But it didn't stop there. Solomon was an avid tennis player. Working with his son Harold, a professional tennis player, he organized a series of annual tennis benefits on behalf of the fight against hunger. In 1983, it was my privilege to watch the likes of Jimmy Connors and John McEnroe play tennis, and to accept a check for forty thousand dollars toward the elimination of hunger in the world. Through their commitment and imagination, Lenny and Harold Solomon have made it possible for people to end hunger by playing tennis.

Valerie Harper

Valerie Harper, Emmy winner for her leading role in the "Rhoda" television series, was one of those attending the March 1977 meeting in which Werner Erhard introduced the Hunger Project. Since then, she has used her public recognition as a vehicle for drawing public attention to the issue of world hunger. In 1980, Harper joined a delegation visiting Somalia at the height of a hunger crisis brought on by drought and an unending war between Somalia and Ethiopia over the contested Ogaden region. Returning to the United States, she addressed the House of Representatives and raised the issue of hunger in East Africa in discussions with countless government officials.

Father Miles Riley

One of the most moving stories from the 1980 trip to Somalia is told by Father Miles Riley, a Roman Catholic priest on the staff of the San Francisco diocese. Riley went to Somalia to find out what the church might do to aid the refugees.

In the course of touring a crowded, dusty refugee camp near the Ethiopian border, Riley was led inside a tiny dark hut. Going from the bright sunshine outside, Riley was at first blind and could only sense a mass of bodies surrounding him. As his vision gradually returned, he found himself in the midst of several mothers, clutching listless, skin-and-bones babies as though hoping their love could take the place of medicine and food.

By the time he could see fully, Riley found himself the focus of all attention in the hut. Was he a doctor? Had he come to save their babies? One desperate mother struggled to her feet and thrust her baby at the priest, saying something Riley couldn't understand.

After devoting his adult life to serving others, the priest took the fragile infant in his arms and found himself crushed by the realization that he had nothing to give. "I wasn't a doctor," he explained. "I had no medicine to administer. I had no food to give." Then his priestly instincts came alive. "I'm often called to minister spiritually to the sick and the dying, and I thought perhaps I should bless the child. But then, I realized that all these people were Moslems." From their point of view, his priestly contribution would be of no value.

The language barrier prevented the priest from even offering words of hope or comfort. He couldn't explain that he was on a fact-finding mission or that he would work for Somalian relief when he returned to the United States. Stripped of all his conventional tools for contributing, Riley found an answer at a more basic human level. "Without thinking, I kissed the baby with all the love and compassion I was feeling right then and gave it back to its mother. Her face burst into the biggest smile you can imagine, and she held her baby up for everyone to see."

John Denver

As I mentioned earlier, John Denver was one of the three principal founders of The Hunger Project in 1977. Since then he has continued to look for ways of making his personal contribution to the end of hunger. It was not surprising, perhaps, that he would write a song, "I Want to Live," to draw popular attention to the problem in a way that showed the human dignity of the hungry rather than holding them up as objects of pity.

Going beyond the obvious, Denver produced a movie on world hunger for use in schools. In large part, the purpose of the film was to eradicate some of the mythology surrounding the problem. As the film documents, hunger persists, it doesn't have to, and individuals will make the difference in ending it.

Denver was also active in bringing the issue of world hunger to the attention of the Carter administration. Later, he served on Carter's Presidential Commission on World and Domestic Hunger.

Pam Jeffcock

For Pam Jeffcock of Columbia Falls, Montana, the commitment to end world hunger took the form of a county-wide food bank. In addition, she was responsible for the creation of a public service announcement to bring the message of ending world hunger to Montana television viewers three times a day. She reports, "The focus of my life has changed. It is something much bigger than myself."

Kenny Rogers

When country singer and composer Kenny Rogers and wife Marianne decided to strike a blow against world hunger, they looked for some way to leverage their contribution. Thus, they donated a million dollars to create "The World Hunger

Awards" to acknowledge the efforts of members of the mass media who draw public attention to the issue of world hunger. Rogers explains:

Marianne and I felt that although one million dollars is a substantial sum of money, it would have little impact by itself on world hunger. We found that recent reports pinpoint public education as the major key to the elimination of hunger. This awards program provided us with the opportunity to effectively encourage, honor and reward . . . those who contribute substantially each year to the education of the public about the issue and its elimination.

Robert Clampitt

Robert Clampitt is publisher of the children's news magazine *Children's Express.* During the crisis in Cambodia, Clampitt supported his young staff in preparing a special *Child for Child Handbook,* giving children suggestions on how they could make a significant contribution to children halfway around the world. The manual gave practical tips on how to bring the message of world hunger to friends, family, school, and community, and advised on project development, fund-raising, and publicity. Quite aside from the contribution made to those starving in Cambodia, Clampitt helped empower a new generation in taking responsibility for their world instead of simply suffering its injustices.

Marguerite Chandler

Marguerite Chandler is a New Jersey wife and mother of two teenage boys. Once she became aware of the problem of world hunger through The Hunger Project, she began looking to see if there was any way an "average" person could make a difference. Here are a few of the answers she found for herself in the first two years of her commitment:

■ She founded a county-wide Food Bank Network to co-ordinate the efforts of the various county agencies involved in feeding people.

■ She has worked with state and county penal systems to give convicts an opportunity to assist in food distribution.

■ She is creating an Aid to Friends program to provide volunteers to assist the handicapped and elderly in preparing their meals.

■ She has worked with local athletic teams to coordinate food drives with games. Five tons of food were collected at one game, for example.

■ She is coordinating a planning committee for a state-wide conference dedicated to ending hunger in New Jersey.

■ She has written and recorded Public Service Announce-ments and distributed them to over six hundred radio sta-tions across the country.

■ She organized a three-week exhibit on ending hunger for the state capitol building and arranged to have leading public officials photographed at the exhibit.

■ She subscribes to a clipping service in order to keep track of articles on hunger in the media; she then redistrib-utes the clippings to other individuals and organizations.

These are only a few of the ways Chandler found she could make a personal contribution to the end of hunger, offering a powerful illustration of personal responsibility in action. Ap-propriately, Chandler was recently named Woman of the Year in her county, and she used that recognition as another vehicle for drawing attention to the problem of hunger.

Raul Julia

Raul Julia, an actor appearing frequently in movies and on television, is best known as a star of numerous Broadway pro-ductions. Concerned with the problem of world hunger, Julia has found numerous ways of pursuing that concern. As one example, theater-goers attending Julia's performances find a surprise in their theater programs. The listing of Julia's theater credits concludes with a lengthy discussion of the problem of world hunger and suggests ways people can contribute to its solution.

Willie Stargell

When Pittsburgh Pirates baseball star Willie Stargell became aware of the problem of hunger, he announced he would find some way of making a special contribution. Later, when he was to be honored for his career in baseball, he asked his Pittsburgh fans to bring cans of food to the stadium for distribution to local food banks.

Harry Chapin

Happily, the list could go on and on, and it grows daily as more and more individuals find ways of taking personal responsibility for the problem of world hunger. I confess a reluctance to stop this reporting, since it means overlooking hundreds and hundreds of genuine heroes.

No one was ever more concerned about world hunger or looked harder to find what he could do than composer-singer Harry Chapin.[3] Throughout the 1960s, Harry devoted himself to a variety of social causes, but he eventually came to the conclusion that there was no greater injustice in the world than could be found in the cases of the hundreds of millions of human beings who went to bed hungry night after night. In 1975, he joined with Father Bill Ayres to form World Hunger Year, an organization dedicated to "give constant and consistent exposure to the hunger problem." From then on, he was to dedicate his professional and personal life to that issue. A substantial proportion of every concert season thereafter was devoted specifically to ending hunger, and Chapin never gave a concert that didn't draw peoples' attention to the problem.

When President Carter appointed a Commission on World and Domestic Hunger, Chapin was an obvious choice as a commissioner. Many observers felt that Chapin was the primary force in getting the commission created in the first place, and he brought a powerful commitment and sense of urgency to the commission's deliberations.

Harry Chapin ran his life according the following principles, which should serve as an undying legacy for us all:

- When in doubt . . . do something.
- I'd rather be wrong than be frightened.
- The key to my life is that I'm willing to make an ass of myself.

When Harry Chapin's life came to a premature end through a heart attack and automobile accident on a Long Island freeway in 1981, there was no one more personally committed to the public interest. In perhaps the world's most appropriate typographical error, the *Washington Post* reported that Harry Chapin died of "a massive heart."

7. ENDING THE NUCLEAR THREAT

Heroism, the Caucasian mountaineers say, is endurance for one moment more.

—George Kennan

Whereas the problem of world hunger has only recently become a compelling personal concern for large numbers of Americans, the threat of thermonuclear extinction has been a real one for more than a generation. Over half our population was born with a nuclear cloud hanging over their heads. From time to time, psychological or sociological studies report interviews with young people who are not seriously planning adult careers, assuming the world will not last that long. For many adults, this is the most shameful legacy we have bestowed on our children.

Like the problem of world hunger, the nuclear threat seems so massive, so complex, that there is nothing an individual can do that would really make a difference. If governments and international bodies cannot solve the problem, what can an average man or woman or child do?

In some respects, the nuclear threat is more difficult to resolve than that of world hunger. Whereas just about everyone would be willing to see hunger end, the consensus is not that clear with regard to nuclear war. While only a few demented souls would wish to see all human life on the planet destroyed, a substantially larger number would be willing to see *some* human life nuked away. There are Americans who would be willing to see a few missiles knock at the door of the Kremlin. There are Arabs who wouldn't object to a nuclear cleansing of Israel.

Moreover, there is an adversarial quality to the nuclear arms race that does not exist in the case of hunger. Once you get beyond the myth that there is not enough food for everyone, it becomes obvious that your well-being and mine is hardly threatened when an Indian or Somalian child is fed rather than left to starve. The nuclear problem is another matter, however. Few believe, for example, that it would be feasible for the U.S. to pull out of the arms race unilaterally. Thus, the solution needs to involve both the U.S. and the U.S.S.R. at the very least.

And while the hunger issue often wallows in a political bog, the nuclear issue has been far more politically cast from the beginning. In 1956, for example, presidential candidate and future U.S. ambassador to the United Nations Adlai Stevenson said, "I believe we should give prompt and earnest consideration to stopping further tests of the hydrogen bomb." Richard Nixon, then the vice president and future president, denounced Stevenson's suggestion as "catastrophic nonsense" and accused him of walking into a "Communist mousetrap." The issue has hardly gotten less politicized in the years since.[1]

Finally, the economic contexts of world hunger and nuclear weapons are importantly different. Whereas a total, global commitment to the elimination of world hunger might mean more work for American farmers, an end to the nuclear arms race would mean closing down the shops of an industry currently doing tens of billions of dollars of business a year. While it can be argued that the nuclear defense industry is not an efficient vehicle for employment and contributes little to the overall quality of life for most Americans, no one denies that calling off the nuclear arms race would require an enormous restructuring of the American economy. A great many people would lose the jobs they now have. Individuals and corporations currently making a great deal of money from the arms race would need to find some other source of income. Inevitably, the vested interests that have established themselves within the nuclear threat represent a powerful obstacle to resolving it.

Given all these complexities, it can easily seem that the problem is unsolvable. It comes as no surprise that the vast majority of us have simply given up. It seems obvious beyond the need for comment that no individual, no matter how concerned or committed, could have an impact. And yet, a great many individuals have nonetheless looked for and found ways to take on the problem. Let's look at a few of them now. While it would be impossible to mention everyone who deserves honoring here —nor have I attempted to limit my examination to the "most important" contributions—there is value in seeing some of the variety of actions individuals have taken.

Helen Caldicott

As an adolescent growing up in Australia, Helen Caldicott was particularly bothered by Nevil Shute's book, *On the Beach,* which dramatized the lingering death of the human race following a nuclear holocaust.[2] Later, during medical school, she was further troubled as she learned more and more about the carcinogenic and mutagenic effects of nuclear radiation. Caldicott and her husband lived in the United States from 1966 to 1969, and she spoke out against nuclear weapons and wrote letters to politicians.

Returning to Australia, Caldicott suffered a nearly fatal case of serum hepatitis, requiring several months in the hospital. In the end she recovered, but the episode had a profound impact on her view of her life. As she was to put it later, "I've been saved to do something. I've been given life. There must be a reason. I knew I had to do something for the planet."

Caldicott's opportunity to "do something for the planet"

came in 1971, when she grew concerned about the dangers of atmospheric nuclear tests being conducted by the French in the Pacific. She testified before the Australian government that radiation from the tests was blowing across Australia, and the point was made effectively enough that the French ultimately gave up their testing program.

When Caldicott returned to live in the United States in 1975, she became active in protests against nuclear power, but soon her chief concern had returned to the issue of nuclear weapons and the threat they pose for the planet.

Throughout her participation in the antinuclear movement, Caldicott has looked to see what she can do specifically as a mother and as a physician. In the former role, for example, she can be found marching in demonstrations, carrying a sign saying, "Babies Die First." Her most potent contributions, however, have been linked to her role as a physician.

In 1978, Caldicott became president of a tiny professional organization: Physicians for Social Responsibility. In that position, she began arguing that physicians will inherit a special burden in the event of nuclear war: the unenviable task of repairing the mutilated and irradiated bodies of the war's survivors. Caldicott's message struck a responsive chord among her fellow physicians throughout the United States. In three years, she saw the organization's membership grow from ten to ten thousand.

Physicians for Social Responsibility, under Helen Caldicott's leadership, has become a mainstay of the movement against nuclear weapons in the 1980s. One of those powerfully moved by PSR's message was Ian Thierman, who felt he could make a contribution by filming a PSR meeting in San Francisco. The resulting film, *The Last Epidemic,* was to become a widely used resource for the antinuclear movement. Some of the film's impact, however, could never have been anticipated.

Bill Perry

Early in the 1980s, students from the University of California at Berkeley and others from the San Francisco Bay Area decided to take their antinuclear protest to the front door of the threat they perceived: the university's Lawrence Livermore Laboratory, where the nation's new nuclear weapons were being developed. A series of demonstrations during 1981 and 1982 resulted in a great deal of mass media coverage and the arrests of many protesters.

During the turbulent 1981–82 period, the head of public relations for Lawrence was Bill Perry.[3] His primary job, most simply put, was to counteract the message being communicated dramatically by the demonstrators. To assist him in that, he formed a speakers bureau to send lab spokespersons into the community to speak—often on the same platform as antinuclear activists.

Over time, Perry heard over and over that his speakers were being upstaged by *The Last Epidemic*. Typically, his speakers would present half an hour of well-reasoned and carefully documented arguments in favor of continued nuclear weapons development. Then their opponents would simply show Thierman's film, describing the holocaust that would follow a nuclear attack, and the lab's cause would be a lost one in audience after audience. Intrigued, Perry arranged to get a copy of film so he could plan strategies to combat it.

One afternoon in April 1982, Bill Perry sat alone in a darkened room to watch *The Last Epidemic*. He would later report that once the film was ended, he sat another two hours alone in the dark, in complete silence, virtually unable to move. He was simply devastated. "It was an awesome moment for me," he would later report. "I realized that nuclear weapons were not simply the next logical step after bombs."

It became clear to Bill Perry that he could no longer continue working at the Lawrence Livermore Lab; he could no longer devote his professional expertise to the defense of nuclear weapons. On May 17, 1982, Bill Perry resigned his post at the lab.

A part of the film's power for Perry lay in a conversation he had had years before. While on a trip to Washington, D.C., he discovered that Helen Caldicott was making a public presentation. Given his position with the Livermore lab, Perry felt he should hear what she had to say. He now recalls being so disturbed by the young physician's presentation that he spoke to her afterward.

"Do you have children?" she asked.

"Yes," he replied.

"What do they ask you about nuclear weapons?"

"They don't ask me anything."

"They will," she predicted.

Sitting in that dark room in 1982, Perry had watched Caldicott once more describing the horrors of the nuclear aftermath in *The Last Epidemic*. Now, their earlier conversation reverberated louder and louder in his memory as he asked and tried to answer his own questions about nuclear weapons.

In their earlier conversation, Caldicott had added, as an aside, "It's too bad you're on the wrong side."

"What do you mean?" Perry had asked. "I'm very good at what I do."

"I'll bet you are," Caldicott rejoined. "That's why I say it's too bad you're on the wrong side." Now, Perry had left the "wrong side" and was on no side at all. He is careful to point out that he did not quit Lawrence Livermore "to go to work for the antinuclear movement." He simply could not continue working on behalf of nuclear weapons.

One day, in the heat of California's debate over Proposition 12, the nuclear freeze initiative, Perry was asked to address a group in Mountain View, in the heart of Silicone Valley and all its defense-industry corporations. Though he was a little reluctant to speak—feeling others were better qualified than he was —Perry agreed.

Perry's first public presentation was greeted by a massive public turnout, as well as a full representation from the media.

In the course of his presentation, Perry realized that he was one of a very small number of people who had actually worked within a nuclear weapons development lab. Most of the experts who spoke in favor of nuclear weapons—not to mention those in opposition—had never been inside such a lab, let alone worked there. He had a special perspective to contribute to the debate, and by election day in November, Perry had made fifty-six speeches.

Bill Perry's experiences offer a special insight into the nature of heroes and how we tend to regard them. At an antinuclear rally one day, Perry was astounded to hear a young folk singer proclaiming the grand achievements of antinuclear hero *Bill Perry.* When Perry introduced himself later, the singer explained his purpose in writing and performing the song. "At certain times in history, people simply need heroes. Most people don't look much like heroes, however, so people like me have to dress them up a bit so they look like heroes."

Perry is currently at work describing his experiences in a book entitled *No Way Out.* To complete the cycle of causality, Helen Caldicott has agreed to write the preface to his book.

Randall Forsberg

During the 1980s in America, resistance to the nuclear arms race has most often been known as the "freeze" movement, centering on the demand that the United States government gain the cooperation of the Soviet Union "to *stop* the testing, production and deployment of nuclear weapons and missiles and new aircraft designed primarily to deliver nuclear weapons." In March 1984, the National Clearinghouse of the Nuclear Weapons Freeze Campaign summed up the record of three years:

> Since March, 1981, when the national campaign began, support for the Freeze has broadened and deepened. The Freeze has been endorsed by 370 city councils, 71 county

councils and 446 town meetings. One or both houses of the legislatures in 23 states have passed freeze resolutions. More than 150 national and international organizations support the Freeze. In the fall of 1982, more than 30% of the American electorate had a chance to vote on the Freeze in 10 states, the District of Columbia and 38 cities and counties. As of June, 1983, there have been 58 state and local freeze referendums; overall, 60% of those voting have favored the Freeze. On May 4, 1983, the U.S. House of Representatives passed a freeze resolution by a vote of 278–149, almost a two-to-one victory.

On June 12, 1982, approximately half a million Americans marched and rallied in New York City on behalf of the freeze, in what has been called the largest peace demonstration in American history. In short, the movement for a nuclear freeze has been a major phenomenon in recent American history, involving tens of millions of Americans, and regarded as significant by and for people around the globe.

The nuclear freeze movement did not "just happen." Someone was responsible for bringing it into existence. That person was not a government official nor a powerful industrialist nor a well-known scholar but a young mother and political science graduate student at MIT.

Randall Forsberg was born in Huntsville, Alabama, the daughter of actor Douglass Watson.[4] She graduated from Columbia's Barnard College in 1965. Two years later she met and married Gunnar Forsberg, and the couple moved to Gunnar's native Sweden. Ms. Forsberg went to work as a typist at the Stockholm International Peace Research Institute. Soon she had risen through the organization's structure, becoming a genuine expert in the field of defense research.

With her divorce in 1974, Ms. Forsberg returned to the United States with her daughter and enrolled in graduate school at MIT, specializing in defense studies within political science. Her studies were to take a powerful turn in 1979, when she was asked to address a group in Louisville, Kentucky. The more she examined ways of stopping the arms race between the U.S. and the U.S.S.R., the more she realized there was nothing to do but simply stop it. *Now.* "Enough is enough," she declared to the Louisville audience. In Forsberg's view, the peace movement had been hampered by too many ideas about what should be done. "I figured that if we all got together for, say, two years and said the same thing, maybe something would happen. The freeze is such an obvious idea."

Leaving Louisville, Forsberg spent the next few months writing a position paper in support of a bilateral nuclear freeze between the U.S. and U.S.S.R.: "Call to Halt the Nuclear Arms Race." In 1980, she organized the Institute for Defense and Disarmament Studies in Brookline, Massachusetts, to support the idea of the freeze. We've already seen some of the indicators of her success.

It is worth noting that Randall Forsberg was not the first person to have the idea of a bilateral nuclear freeze. If nothing else, I know *I* had that idea at least a hundred times and even said it to someone at least half that often. What was special about Forsberg was her willingness to take responsibility for making it a reality. As Senator Edward Kennedy described her achievement: Randall Forsberg "galvanized the nation on an issue where so many others had almost lost hope."

Harold Willens

While Randall Forsberg deserves credit for stepping forward and sounding the call for a national movement to create a nuclear freeze, simply sounding the call was not sufficient. For the movement to have the impact it has had, hundreds of thousands of individuals have had to look for and act on the forms of participation particularly appropriate to them. When the California Bilateral Nuclear Weapons Freeze Initiative passed with the approval of some 4 million voters on November 2, 1982, no individual was more responsible than businessman Harold Willens.[5]

Willens is an unlikely hero in the antiwar movement, as he himself concedes:

> If anyone has great cause to "hate the Russians," I am that person. I was born in Russia and during my childhood experienced the terror of the Bolshevik Revolution. My recollections of life there still return in occasional nightmares. One such dream brings back memories of watching several drunken soldiers force their way into our tiny house and hearing them threaten to kill us all if we did not give them money and a few other things. In another periodic dream, I smell the smoke and stare with sickened sadness at the flames of nearby homes set afire by a band of marauders.

Willens's family escaped from Russia illegally in 1922 and came to the United States, where Willens was to become totally devoted to his new home. It was perfectly natural that the young Willens would serve with the U.S. Marine Corps during World War II. Trained in the Japanese language, intelligence officer Willens was sent to both Hiroshima and Nagasaki shortly after the end of the war. There, at the sites of the only two uses of nuclear weapons against human beings, Willens witnessed the horrors of nuclear war firsthand. It was an experience he would never forget.

By 1960, Harold Willens had returned to civilian life and had proven his mastery of free enterprise with big successes in textiles and real estate. His newly achieved financial well-being gave Willens some breathing space in which to find a way "to give something back to the country that had given me the great gift of the good life." At a seminar presented by the Center for the Study of Democratic Institutions in Santa Barbara, California, Willens found himself thrust into a several-days-long discussion of the nuclear arms race. He recalled his experiences in Hiroshima and Nagasaki and found he had discovered the contribution he must make to the country of his birth and his country of adoption.

As Willens looked for ways to make this contribution, it seemed to him that he should focus his efforts within the business community. He was a businessman, after all, and a successful one to boot. Thus, during the Vietnam agony, Willens cofounded and chaired an organization called Business Executives Move for Vietnam Peace. Later, he would recall with pleasure President Johnson's frustration at not being able to dismiss the new antiwar group as "soft-headed" or "soft on communism," terms with which he was fond of dismissing college student protesters. Willens had mobilized opposition to the Vietnam war from within the bosom of American capitalism.

When the bilateral nuclear freeze movement became a national reality, it was natural for Willens to chair the campaign in California. He raised millions of dollars in support of the campaign, coordinated the collection of signatures needed to put the freeze initiative on the California ballot, and generally lobbied for support among California's voters. On November 2, 1982, his efforts were rewarded with success.

Marianne Hamilton
Polly Mann

Marianne Hamilton and Polly Mann were two friends living in Minnesota who found themselves talking increasingly about the dangers of nuclear war and the inability of the American people in general to deal with that threat in an effective way.[6] Finally, they decided it was time for *them* to take action.

In January 1982, Hamilton and Mann organized a conference of local women to explore what they could do to avert the threat of nuclear extinction. By the time the conference was completed, the 115 women in attendance had created WAMM:

Women Against Military Madness, "dedicated to changing our government's spending from war to a healthy society."

Rather than focusing on a single line of action, WAMM has encouraged women to find their own ways of acting against the nuclear threat: both individually and in concert. WAMM member Moira Moga explains this way:

> We recognize that the first steps anyone takes are often the hardest. We help each other by respecting each other's choices. Everyone will say and do what is appropriate for her.

WAMM members have demonstrated along Minnesota highways and have sent delegations to march in other cities. Some members meet regularly to plan correspondence with public officials and to write and send letters. Six women brought their families together as a team to create a slide show that draws the connections between military weapons and war toys for children.

Avan Mattison

In 1945, at just about the time the United Nations charter was being signed in San Francisco, a four-year-old Avan Mattison in Pasadena had a powerful vision in which she saw her planet facing a time of great decision: facing an ultimate choice between war and peace. She saw herself serving as a "pathfinder" in the quest for peace and would spent the rest of her life looking for ways of translating her vision into reality.

During 1961–62, for example, she was drawn to the various efforts at détente being pursued within the U.S. State Department, the Organization of American States, and other organizations, but she was also struck by the lack of a coherent context for those efforts. Everyone seemed to be going in different directions with nothing to bring them together.

Then, in 1980, Costa Rica spearheaded a proposal in the United Nations to proclaim 1985 the International Year of Peace. In a rare moment of accord, the General Assembly voted unanimously in favor of the proposal. For Mattison, this action could represent another empty gesture or something really powerful.

As she looked for ways she could make the International Year of Peace something more than just words, Mattison discovered that various individuals and organizations have honored the opening of the General Assembly's sessions each year since 1945. At Assisi, for example, chapel bells are rung each year at the precise moment that the General Assembly convenes.

Mattison now saw the possibility of bringing the people of the world together to honor the possibility of peace. What a powerful experience it would be for all humankind, she imagined, if there were a worldwide "minute of silence" as the UN convened in 1985, followed by a joyous "moment of sound."

In 1983, she formally incorporated Pathways To Peace under the general principle that "individuals, acting in concert with one another, *do* make a difference in the quality of our lives, our institutions, our environments, our planetary future." One of Pathways' projects was to create a test run of the "Minute of Silence—Moment of Sound" idea in a single city—San Francisco—when the UN General Assembly convened on September 18, 1984. Whatever was learned in San Francisco in 1984 would be used in planning a worldwide celebration in 1985.

Now the dream became a matter of hard work. Clearly one person could not pull it off, so Mattison began enrolling friends in the project. Existing peace groups, churches, corporations, and other organizations were contacted and asked to support the project. Public officials were invited to make the event an official one. Local media people began planning how to use their facilities to bring the celebration to the whole community.

As I write this, the 1984 San Francisco event is still being created. By the time you read this, it will have happened. Whatever the outcome of the project, it stands as a powerful example of the difference an individual can make on behalf of us all.

Mary Earle

Mary Earle is a writer living in Mill Valley, California, just north of the Golden Gate Bridge out of San Francisco. In 1982 she was asked to join in the writing of a book on the nuclear arms race. Taking the job required her to "delve into mounds of material I knew existed but had never wanted to read. Like most everyone I know, I simply did not want to think about nuclear war."

The more she read, the more Earle's worst fears were confirmed. Had she withdrawn from the book project, everyone involved would have no doubt been understanding. She wouldn't have been the first person to flee from something that painful to confront. Instead, she chose to redouble her efforts, to make the book as powerful as possible in communicating the dangers she saw to a broader audience.

Soon Earle had taken on a personal responsibility for bringing an end to the threat of nuclear war. But what to do? She found one answer in an experience she had had years before, and soon began writing to all her friends. Her letter began:

About 18 years ago, when I was in college, I received a long single-spaced letter like this that had a very profound impact on my life. An acquaintance of mine had addressed his friends and associates about the war that was then escalating in Vietnam. I knew very little about what was actually occurring in Vietnam and had accepted the view that it was our rightful role to fight communism in this struggling democracy. The letter told me another side of the story. Several months later, I was at the center of campus opposition to the war, speaking, writing, and demonstrating, talking to everyone I knew about the deceptions and dangers of U.S. policy.

Remembering that letter, I write to you now to share with you the other side of what we hear from our government and in the media about nuclear war and the arms race. . . .

John Marks

In 1981, the Union of Concerned Scientists created the Arms Control Program to organize campus teach-ins around the country. John Marks, a former foreign service officer, was hired to tour the country and meet with activists in the peace movement, academics, public officials, experts in national security, and others.[7] On November 11, 1981, as a result of UCS's organizing efforts, more than 150 teach-ins were held.

In the course of his work with the Arms Control Program, Marks became aware of the ways in which divisions of opinion within the peace movement got in the way of establishing a broad-based public commitment to ending the nuclear threat. Rather than creating a super-organization to include all points of view, Marks concluded it might be more useful to establish a network of activities appropriate to the variety of interests that might be mobilized for a common purpose.

The Nuclear Network was thus created on the basis of two fundamental propositions: "Nuclear war is totally unacceptable," and "Ordinary people have the power to prevent it." To turn those propositions into reality, the Network initiated a variety of projects, including:

■ an organization of business executives working against nuclear war;

■ a Children's Nuclear Disarmament Network;

■ a Public Interest Video Network;

■ a conference on the psychological roots of the arms race.

In an interview with Mark Satin of *Renewal,* John Marks described the operating principle of the Network this way:

> You've got to show people there are things they can do to make a difference. Each of us can do *some*thing! Each of us can take responsibility.

Gerald Jampolsky

For nearly a decade, The Center for Attitudinal Healing in Tiburon, California, has been serving children with catastrophic illnesses by bringing them together to share experiences and to support each other. From the start, the center's founder, Gerald Jampolsky, was struck by the wisdom and clarity that children bring to their experience of the world. He was so impressed, in fact, that he began taking children around the country to talk to radio and TV audiences about love and peace.[8]

During the Falkland Islands fighting between Britain and Argentina, Jampolsky asked some children in a Colorado school what they would do if they could talk to the leaders involved. As he reported to interviewer Peggy Taylor:

> The answers were extraordinary. Their remarks made me high as a kite. The children have hope; it's we adults who say things like "There just always have to be wars."

Jampolsky was so moved by his experience with the children in that Colorado school that he wrote to children all over the country, asking them what they thought should be done to achieve peace. Within five weeks, he had received thirty-five hundred responses. Some of the children drew pictures, some wrote poems, some wrote letters to public officials, like this one from a ten-year-old girl:

Dear Mr. President,

I wrote befor to you butt nothing seems to be happening for one of the reasons I am writing to you is because I really ment what I said about not having Nuclear war when I watched you on tv when I was sick you just turned your head when it came to That I hope this time it works.

Hannah Beth Watson

A selection of the children's submissions were soon published and Jampolsky was traveling around the country sharing the book with public officials, scholars, and others. Soon conferences and other events were being organized around this theme, which had become Jampolsky's life work. By now, the book's title had become the general name of his work: *Children as Teachers of Peace.*

Samantha Smith

Samantha Smith was an eleven-year-old fifth grader living in the small town of Manchester, Maine. Her response to the nuclear threat was to write personal letters to President Regan and to Yuri Andropov asking them to do whatever was necessary to avert war. The Soviet leader responded personally, assuring her that "we in the Soviet Union are trying and doing everything we can so that there will be no war between our two countries." Acknowledging her honesty and courage, moreover, he invited her to visit the Soviet Union with her parents. Both the exchange of letters and Samantha's subsequent visit to Russia drew wide public attention to the problem, as did a subsequent trip to Hiroshima to deliver a copy of the television documentary *The Day After* to a peace conference.

Archbishop John Quinn

On October 4, 1981, many San Franciscans celebrated the eight hundredth anniversary of the city's namesake: St. Francis of Assisi. Prominent among the celebrants was San Francisco's Roman Catholic archbishop, John Quinn.[9] Addressing a congregation of parishioners, Quinn spoke out against the nuclear arms race as a "crime against God and humankind."

> A "just" war is a contradiction in terms. Nuclear weapons are not simply conventional weapons on a large scale. They are qualitatively of a whole different order of destructiveness. . . . Nuclear weapons and the arms race must be condemned as immoral.

Quinn's stunned congregation rose spontaneously to their feet and applauded him.

In the months to come, Quinn was to take a number of concrete steps to back up his publicly stated conviction. He appointed special diocesan workers to take on the task of educating San Francisco's parishes and parochial schools on the facts of the nuclear arms race and on California's nuclear freeze proposition. In addition, he began playing an active role in raising the nuclear issue among his fellow bishops.

Sister Frances Russell

Sister Frances Russell is a Sisters of Charity nun living in Cheyenne, Wyoming, home of Warren Air Force Base, which is slated to be an MX missile site.[10] Much of her work has been as a social worker, settling refugees in American cities. She has been responsible, for example, for finding homes for Cuban refugees in Cheyenne.

While her work with Cuban refugees and with other needy members of the community has been generally accepted, other activities have made Russell a generally despised figure in Cheyenne. Simply put, she regards the nuclear arms race as immoral and has felt she must act in accord with her religious views. Every Friday she leads a group of clergy and laypeople to the fence surrounding the base, and the group prays for peace. In return, she has received death threats, people have spat on her as she walked down the street, and on at least one occasion a police officer shook his fist in her face and warned, "We'll get you."

In a very different response, Russell was named Social Worker of the Year by the National Association of Social Workers. Living on subsistence wages from her order and unable to get work in Cheyenne, Russell announced she would give half the five-hundred-dollar award to fight world hunger and the other half to oppose the MX missiles.

The Refusal of Civil Defense

Given the undeniable threat of nuclear war, what could be more logical and incontestable than planning ways to mute its impact? It's not surprising that the beginning of the arms race in the 1950s also saw a national mania for building bomb shelters. Government publications were issued, instructing children to cover their faces as soon as they saw the nuclear fireball.

Over the years, interest in civil defense waned. Few people built bomb shelters, government civil defense measures became increasingly low-key. About the only reminder most Americans had were the periodic "tests of the Emergency Broadcast System" on the radio. After all, "détente" had become a more popular word than "holocaust."

All this was to change with the arrival of the Regan administration, with its enlarged military budgets and talk of combating "the evil empire." In language reminiscent of *Dr. Strangelove,* military and civilian strategists began discussing ways of winning a nuclear war. In one estimate, a good civil defense program could reduce American deaths from 80 percent of the population to "as low as 40 percent." The Federal Emergency Management Administration, accordingly, advised local municipalities to prepare plans for evacuating their civilian populations to safer areas in the event of a nuclear attack. Some public officials, such as California Senator Alan Cranston, call the whole thing "a cruel and dangerous hoax that encourages the false notion that nuclear war is . . . tolerable and perhaps even winnable."

In California's Marin County, just north of San Francisco, the Board of Supervisors instructed Dr. Richard Ridenour, Director of Health and Human Services, to study the consequences of a nuclear attack on San Francisco and advise on evacuation strategies. Ridenour undertook the job with a "hopeful attitude" and set about studying the federal government's relocation plans. The more he learned about the amount of damage that was likely to result from a nuclear attack on San Francisco, the more Ridenour became convinced that his task was a hopeless one.

For the purpose of his study, Ridenour had assumed a twenty-megaton bomb being detonated one thousand meters above the TransAmerica building near the center of San Francisco. In Sausalito, just across the Golden Gate Bridge from San Francisco and facing it across the bay, it was estimated that virtually everyone would be killed instantly in the initial explosion. Moving north from Sausalito, it was estimated that half of Mill Valley's residents would die in the initial explosion, and the rest would either die of injuries in the next two days or of radiation sickness within two weeks.

Moving farther north, Ridenour reported on the prospects for Novato and its community hospital.

> Novato Community Hospital, farther from the core at 18 miles, sheltered by a hill, would survive with moderate damage. But from the city of Novato alone, the commu-

nity hospital would be faced with the care of 5,000 serious injuries, having no electricity after 48 hours, no water after 12 hours, no telephones, no linen after 8 hours, no medical supplies after 12 hours. At this time 5,000 new cases of radiation sickness would start to come in. The building could not hold more than 100 patients.

Ridenour reported his findings to the Board of Supervisors. At the December 1, 1981, meeting of the board, Supervisor (now Congresswoman) Barbara Boxer pointed out that civilian evacuation would only work if there were a "sufficient warning." In a nuclear attack, however, we would have no more than a thirty-minute warning at best. She also commented on medical estimates of the casualties likely to result from an attack on the San Francisco area. "The bottom line," Boxer concluded, "is that there's no way we can evacuate skeletons."

At its March 16, 1982, meeting, Boxer arranged for the Board of Supervisors to watch Ian Thierman's film, *The Last Epidemic.* Afterward, Boxer and fellow supervisor Gary Giacomini proposed that Marin County refuse to develop an evacuation plan. Instead, following the example of Cambridge, Massachusetts, they proposed that the county prepare and distribute a pamphlet warning residents of the dangers of nuclear war and urging them to take actions to avert it. The proposal passed, and the pamphlet, published in May, began:

> When the Federal Emergency Management Administration (FEMA) announced that it wanted every city and county to prepare a nuclear evacuation plan, Marin county administrative staffers dutifully went to work. They went as far as a draft plan that envisioned Marin residents huddling for safety in the Waldo Tunnel before the essential absurdity of the undertaking struck them. Pressure from a nuclear blast in San Francisco, they learned, would blow people out of the tunnel like a shot from a cannon.

The pamphlet then proceeded to describe the nature of the nuclear threat and ended with a list of suggestions for what citizens could do and provided the names and addresses of public officials, newspapers, and radio and television stations.

Individuals and Groups

In concluding these examinations of individuals working to end world hunger and the threat of nuclear war, I want to make clear that my purpose has not been to heap credit on a few individuals and ignore the contributions of the many people not mentioned above. In those cases where I interviewed the people I've discussed, they were usually quite insistent on making sure I didn't think they had "done it all." Most spoke at length of the importance of "individuals acting in concert," to use Avan Mattison's term.

Without ignoring or denying the obvious necessity of many people involving themselves in the solution of big problems, it is nonetheless my specific purpose in this book to point to the importance of individual responsibility within that context. First, what becomes a big social movement almost always begins with one person being willing to step forward. While millions of people have made contributions to the nuclear freeze movement, for example, all those responsibilities were only possible because Randall Forsberg was willing to take personal responsibility for it at the outset.

The second point I want to make in this regard is a little more difficult to grasp. Social movements will be truly potent to the extent that the individuals participating in them are willing to act from a sense of personal responsibility for the whole, even if they weren't the first to speak out. This is what has made research for these two chapters so profoundly moving. In a world where people so often seem committed to taking credit, I found a very large number of individuals willing to be responsible purely on the basis of their commitment rather than out of a desire for personal publicity.

8. THE OPPORTUNITIES ARE EVERYWHERE

Those persons who are burning to display heroism may rest assured that the course of social evolution will offer them every opportunity.

—Havelock Ellis

In a way, this book had its beginning in a Honolulu shopping center several years ago. My son Aaron and I had gone there one noon to watch some friends of ours, a popular singing couple, perform at an outdoor stage.

As showtime approached, a few hundred shoppers had gathered for the performance in a semicircle formed about ten feet from the stage and on the second-level balcony overlooking the stage. There was a really festive mood in the crowd, since the couple, Leon and Malia, were well-loved in Hawaii.

A minute or two before Leon and Malia were to come onstage, it happened. Someone on the second-level balcony dropped a box of popcorn. The box fell into the area between the downstairs audience and the stage. It hit, fell on its side, and some of the popcorn spilled out on the ground, messing up an otherwise clean area.

A hush fell over the crowd as hundreds of eyes focused on the intruding popcorn box. Though no one seemed to say anything, you could hear their thoughts. "Must have been a hippie." "Parents should watch their children more carefully." "Probably a tourist." The whole mood of the gathering was destroyed in a matter of seconds.

Without thinking, I performed an antisocial act. Stepping out of the downstairs crowd, I walked across the opening toward the stage, bent down, scooped the spilled popcorn into the box, and carried the box to a nearby trash can. Altogether, it probably took twenty to thirty seconds, but it was one of the longest hours of my life.

When I stood up with the box of popcorn, I found the entire audience staring at me. They continued staring all the way to the trash can, and when I returned to my son in the crowd, I found myself disowned. Quickly whispering, "Why did you *do* that?" Aaron moved away from me, pretending to be with someone else in the crowd.

All told, it was an embarrassing experience for both of us, and it troubled me for days. Essentially it came down to this: Why did I feel so bad for doing something good? I didn't expect to be carried through the shopping center on the shoulders of adoring followers. I didn't expect a good citizenship medal or even applause. But why did my simple act seem so unacceptable? That question was to stay with me and reappear.

Shortly after the Great Popcorn Caper, I found myself teaching a course in Social Problems at a University of Hawaii summer school session. Now summer school at the University of Hawaii is a mixed undertaking. Some of the students enroll in summer school in order to earn the credits needed to graduate early. Others use summer school to make up deficiencies from the regular school year. And some students from mainland universities find it intellectually imperative to pursue their studies in Honolulu during the summer.

Whatever their reasons, about fifty students chose to take Social Problems that summer. Since I had been expecting five or six students, I had to make a number of last-minute adjustments in the course. In particular, I decided to grade students on the basis of two multiple-choice exams instead of the term papers and essay exams I had originally planned. After the mid-term exam, however, I found myself with a problem.

Several students, unhappy with the grades they had gotten on the exam, asked if they could do any additional work in the course as a way of raising their grades. Several suggested writing term papers, and I said I would think about it.

As I considered the prospect of wading through piles of student prose on such uplifting topics as racism, war, rape, and mayhem, my support for the term paper solution dissolved. Instead, I began a discussion with the class regarding their motivations for taking a course in social problems. Quickly we decided that simply learning about the seamy side of society was a sick way to spend the summer. Ultimately, we concluded that the only justifiable purpose for learning about social problems would be to solve them. That laid the groundwork for the extra-credit course project that several hundred students in various courses were to undertake in the years to follow.

The extra-credit course project was simple enough to state: "Find a social problem and fix it." The assignment was so different from anything the students had been asked to do in a college course before that I found I had to spell out what would *not* qualify:

■ No credit would be given for drawing my attention to a problem I might not be aware of.
■ No credit would be given for finding out who was to blame for a particular problem.
■ No credit would be given for bitching about how bad things are.
■ No credit would be given for telling me what Weber, Durkheim, or other great sociologists would say about the problem.

Finally, it was not sufficient to attack the problem, to make a dent in it, to give it the "good ole college try." I warned students I would not be impressed if they gave up all their other courses to devote their lives to the problem they had chosen. The bottom line would always be the same: "Did you solve it?" In this vein, I suggested they not take on world hunger, racism in America, or the threat of thermonuclear war as their course projects.

I told them to find problems that were "social"—something that bothered others as well as themselves. And as a fortunate afterthought, I told them they couldn't get credit for solving problems they created. I told them about the Great Popcorn Caper as an example.

The remainder of that course in social problems provided the most rewarding experience in my career as a professor. Fifty students set out to fix the world, and fix it they did. The result was so moving to me that I have made it available in every course I've taught since then. By now, hundreds of students have reported to me on the projects they've done in connection with my courses. I want to share some of their experiences with you to demonstrate the variety of opportunities for heroism all around us today.

One young man chose to take on a problem that actually plagues most American cities today: potholes in the street. In his case, there was one particular pothole. It was located at an intersection near his home, and he said it had been there for as long as he could remember. Most of the residents of the area had gotten accustomed to swerving around it, and newcomers learned about it the hard way. Clearly, the pothole was not simply an annoyance but was downright dangerous. So my student decided to do something about it.

Impressing his brother into service, he stopped in at a hardware store located on the intersection to buy sand and cement. Once the store owner learned what the young men were planning to do, he loaned them a shovel and a concrete mixer, let them use his water, and threw in his own son as additional labor. The three young men started work.

As soon as they began filling in the pothole, several passing motorists parked their cars and began directing traffic around the workers. Then some passing children made up "Wet Concrete" signs to be arranged around the pothole once the work was done. Altogether, about twenty neighbors participated in the project. Together, they had handled a problem that had bothered them all for years. All it took was someone who was willing to step forward and be responsible for it happening.

Here's a different example. One of my students explained to me that she was somewhat disappointed by college life. She had looked forward to making new friends at college and having a good time with them. Instead, she said, her dorm was simply a place where strangers slept. No one seemed to know anyone else, nor, for that matter, to care. While they might occasionally nod to one another in the hallways, that was it. My student felt that her disappointment was shared by others living in the dorm, and she set out to do something about it.

Her idea was to organize a dorm cookout. She prepared posters and sign-up sheets for the cookout and put them up in the bathrooms on each floor of the dorm. She said she felt kind of nervous and embarrassed about doing it, since nobody had put her in charge of the dorm's social life; she also was afraid the other residents would think the idea was hokey. Three days later, nobody had signed up for the cookout.

What I like most about this story is that it puts the lie to our notion about the first step being the hardest in any undertaking. Actually, the second step is the hardest.

Since no one had signed up for the cookout, my student had every reason to drop the idea. She had tried, after all. She went to the trouble of making up the posters and sign-up sheets. If nobody wanted to have a social life in the dorm, that was too bad for them. The possibilities for self-righteous one-liners were endless. My student did something else—something absolutely heroic.

Stopping another girl in the hallway, she asked "Have you seen the cookout posters in the johns?" She had. "I'm the one who put them up. Don't you think it would be fun to all get together for a cookout? We can get to know each other, listen to some music, and just have a good time. Wouldn't that be fun?" Once the other girl admitted it sounded like a good idea, my student closed the deal: "Would you be willing to put your name on the signup sheet?" With one name on the signup sheet, she found someone else, enrolled her in the idea of the cookout, and got another name on the list. After she had personally enrolled four or five girls, the tide turned. People started signing up of their own accord. Soon, all the lists were full. My student was getting phone calls from people volunteering to bring records, stereos, and the like.

By the day of the cookout, most of the girls in the dorm already knew each other. They had a glorious time together, and before it was over, one girl had volunteered to organize an ice cream party, and another was organizing a taco party. My student could report that her dorm now operated like a large family—it had become exactly what she had expected when she arrived at college.

It's important to recognize that something more profound than college partying is involved in this example. Quite aside from the cookout and other parties, the quality of life in the dorm was profoundly altered: strangers had become family. Moreover, there is a good likelihood that the experience of being a large family would be passed on from student generation to generation in the dorm.

It's also important to note that the transformation of dorm life was brought about by one person—a young woman with no special skills in community organization, no past history of such activities, and certainly no formal responsibility or authority in the matter. All she possessed was the willingness and courage to do the job.

Litter-Picking

Picking up litter seems to be the most obvious example of a social problem that my students can fix, and a large percentage of the projects report that activity. It usually comes about when a student finds a mess that he or she doesn't like, realizes that no one else is going to clean it up, and just handles it. Very often, they discover that it's not all right with the rest of the world for people to take personal responsibility for public things. Here's a typical example.

> *Describe the social problem.* Pollution. Went to Ala Moana Beach to swim and get a tan with my friends. The wind started blowing and all these paper cups, papers, and soda cans came rolling our way. My friends started complaining in disgust.
> *Describe what you did.* So I got up and started picking them up and threw them away in the garbage cans.
> *Describe the reactions of others who saw you doing it.* My friends said I was dumb and said to leave it to the City and County to clean it up since we were paying them for it. (I didn't tell them it was for a project.) As for other people, they just looked at me and smiled; some just turned away.

Or consider this young woman who also decided to pick up trash at Ala Moana Beach Park. Reporting that she "kept picking until one section of the beach looked as though trash had never laid eyes on the sand," she appears to have provoked virtually every possible reaction in those around her.

> Well, some of the people just smiled at me as though I was some good samaritan doing her duty, some of the people gave me a smirk as though I was paying for something that I had done, and some of the small kids even followed me and picked up trash with me. But most of the people just looked and went on with what they were doing as though they were saying whatever turns you on!

Disbelief often strikes innocent bystanders when my students go to work. One student decided to clean up the broken glass in a street near her house—left there by an earlier auto accident. She wanted to do it so she could walk barefoot in the area.

Enlisting her brother into the project, she set to work with a broom and dustpan.

This one lady was planning to make a left-hand turn, and when it was clear for her to go she just sat in the car and kept staring at us. This other man honked his horn. And this policeman gave me a weird look.

Quite often people find that sort of behavior puzzling. If someone were to discover you cleaning up some mess in public, they would automatically assume: (1) you made the mess and got caught; (2) you made the mess and got a guilty conscience; (3) you didn't make the mess, but you're being punished for doing something else just as bad. As a last resort, people will be forced to assume that *you must be stealing garbage.* Try telling someone that you just didn't like to look at the mess, so you decided to clean it up. It is likely that you will produce disbelief in the person you are talking to. "Sure, you just decided to clean it up." "What's really in it for you?" "Am I on 'Candid Camera'?"

Consider this project, somewhat similar to litter-picking:

I live on a ridge and the drive up to the top is very pretty. From the bottom until you reach the houses, there are two rows of flowering trees planted in front of a lava rock wall. Recently, someone wrote the word "Kimo's" in big white letters on the wall. Every time I drove past it, I noticed how bad it looked, and I assumed that the gardeners would do something about it. But nobody did. I am sure they realized how bad it looked but didn't want to get involved. My parents agreed that it looked bad, so I got some paint thinner and a brush and took it off. I couldn't get it all off, but if you didn't know it was there, you wouldn't notice it. As I was brushing it off, people who drove by just looked at me and smiled. I am sure they thought I was the one who wrote it. It really looks much better now, and I am glad I did it.

Of course, everyone would assume that only Kimo would go to the trouble of removing the mess. After all, Kimo made the mess. He's the one who should remove it. That's only fair and just. Why would anyone else do it? Right?

Consider the experience of a student who got fed up with all the trash and beer bottles in the parking lot at a beach he frequented. He got out of his car and began picking up beer bottles and trash and throwing them in the rubbish can.

People having little parties started staring at me and one guy even started picking up his rubbish bag. Then a funny thing happened. A cop pulled in and everyone started to leave, because drinking alcoholic beverages on public grounds is illegal. Anyway, the policeman pulls up next to me and asks me what do you you think you're doing?! And I casually told him that I was cleaning up the park. He looked at me in a funny way and told me just to leave it and go home.

Actually, things are not quite as bad as I've painted them. My students have not always gotten negative feedback for cleaning up someone else's mess. I'm pleased to report that there are humans among us who simply accept responsible behavior at face value and support it. Here's one student's experience:

Shortly after the extra-credit project was assigned, I had a chance to go on a hike with the Hawaii Trail and Mountain Hiking Club into Kuliouou Valley. I brought along a hefty garbage bag to pick up litter along the way. I noticed litter at the beginning of the trail, so I returned earlier from the hike than the others to pick up that litter. There were mainly beer cans. As I started to collect the trash, another lady had also returned early from the hike. She noticed what I was doing and pitched in, saying "You're one of those rare people." I explained to her that I was doing this for an extra-credit project. She was surprised to hear that this project was for a sociology class rather than an environmental one. She was also kind enough to take my picture for proof of my deed. Ultimately, we cleaned the litter, which ended that problem hopefully for a while. Besides being able to help clean the environment a little, I also met that little ol' lady who was also concerned about solving social problems.

Another hiker, on another hike, reports a similar experience:

I found that by picking up the rubbish the problem was no longer there. I had just bagged a social problem. Another result was that one of my friends saw me picking up the rubbish and decided that he could solve social problems, too! So now there are at least two of us up there in the mountains solving social problems.

The more I have read reports of others joining in, the clearer it has become that most people would be willing to clean up the litter they find in public places—except for what they fear others would think of them. The social agreements that constrain us are often just too strong. Yet, when one person breaks through the agreements and takes responsibility anyway, that revolutionary act suddenly makes it safer for others to do what they really want to do.

It takes courage to break with convention and assume a personal responsibility for having the world work the way you want it to work. You just never know how it's going to turn out. You may find yourself becoming a leader of a social movement, a hero of social reform; or you may find yourself simply looking silly. That's the risk, and it's not as trivial as it sounds when you are simply reading about it.

Let's look at some other situations in which students have found they can make a difference.

Neighborhood Problems

How many times have you been walking along the sidewalk and found your way challenged by a hydraulic sentry. I know you've run into something like this sprinkler that a student reports was "sprinkling the lawn, the sidewalk, and the right lane of Dole Street." What do you do in a situation like that?

My student reports that pedestrians crossed to the other side of the street. Motorists swerved to the left lane to avoid getting drenched by the sprinkler. My student, on the other hand, simply moved the sprinkler. The problem was solved and life continued.

Many are the hazards of walking along sidewalks. Once you make it past the sprinklers, you are confronted by the branches of overgrown trees and branches. One student suffered through this problem at the entrance to a cafeteria on campus until finally, tired of being slapped in the face, she decided to break off the worst branch. Two friends saw what she was doing and joined in. Working together, they quickly had the tree trimmed so that it didn't obstruct the walkway. When her friends thanked her for starting the job, she asked them why they had never done it. This is her report:

> They both replied that because it bothered everyone, they expected someone else to do something about it. It seems that people rely on someone else to do things that would benefit everyone.

When another student found her way blocked by a small tree, she checked it out and discovered it had been loosened by heavy rains and was on the verge of toppling over across the sidewalk. Getting a hammer, stake, and cord, she spent about ten minutes and anchored the tree firmly. Now she gets to pass by her handiwork every day going to her bus stop. Every day she gets a reminder that she makes a difference in the world. Here's a different, though common, bush problem:

> On the corner of an intersection in our neighborhood, there was a very tall bush. So whenever you wanted to cross the intersection, you couldn't see if both sides were clear because the bush was blocking the view on one side. You would have to slowly move forward, until your car was sticking out a little in the middle of the intersection, to see. Thus, many accidents had occurred because of this bush.

That's the sort of problem that people put up with forever. This time it was different, however. This student simply got out his clipping shears and trimmed the bush back. Now his neighbors can see when they come to the intersection and the risk of accidents is reduced.

Sometimes you can't simply handle a problem by yourself. It may be necessary to get someone else to handle it. Often you must get someone else to do the job they are paid to do. Thus, numerous students report calling government officials to have trees and bushes trimmed, abandoned cars removed, and so forth. Often, simply placing a call to the right office will handle it. And just as often, it won't. Sometimes you must be doggedly persistent.

One student who lives beside a golf course reported that the overgrown grass and weeds on the edges of the course often caught fire during dry spells, thereby endangering nearby homes. She decided to visit the groundskeeper at the course. She talked to him about the fire hazard. She offered to cut the grass and weeds herself if that's what it would take. The groundskeeper said he'd do something, but he didn't. She returned. Still nothing happened. She returned with her father. She kept after the groundskeeper until he finally handled the problem, and the student now reports that the grass and weeds are kept cut. She says this of the experience: "I realize that the groundskeeper was aware of the problem because of the previous fires, and undoubtedly other people probably tried to get the areas cut, but I actually handled it. For this reason, I feel very pleased and proud." Sometimes my students have qualms about what they have done, though they are pretty sure they have acted appropriately. One found a problem where the traffic department was installing traffic lights.

One pole that is not complete yet is about face high. Sticking out of it is a five foot piece of thick wire and it blocks the whole sidewalk at about face level. To keep from getting blinded, people are ducking under it and around it into the street where it is a hazard to both people & cars.

I walked under it and grabbed it from behind and twisted it away from people's faces. Then I stuffed the whole thing back into the pole where it belonged. I secured it inside so it would not come out again. The traffic department may not be happy, but our neighborhood is.

My friend said I was a vandal.

Question: Is it unlawful to bend a piece of metal for the safety of the people, at the expense of the Traffic Commission? I think not. It is much cheaper to buy new wire than a new eye!

Traffic Problems

If sprinklers and tree branches are an annoyance to pedestrians, highway obstructions can be downright dangerous. And the obstructions are many and varied.

On a fast-moving, usually speeding road, people were suddenly braking and tooting their horns to avoid a fallen branch in one of the lanes.

About twenty yards before the Koko Head Avenue cut-off, in the right lane, there was a pretty big board lying right in the center, so cars were swerving partly into the center lane to avoid it.

A two-week-old kitten was on a busy street. Lost and afraid, it just sat there in the middle of the road. From afar, it looked like just a piece of rubbish so other drivers before me weren't cautious upon approaching the kitten. Only when they were a few feet away, then they realized it was a kitten and slowed down and swerved off the road or changed lanes.

The first report was from a pedestrian. When traffic eased up, she darted onto the highway and dragged the branch to the side of the road. Her sister said, "You're weird!" The second report was from a student motorist. He pulled to the side of the freeway, waited for a break in the traffic, and pulled the board to the side. What makes the second story particularly telling is that he had simply swerved and passed by the board the day before. It was still lying there in the middle of the freeway a day later—waiting for someone to do something about it.

The two-week-old kitten was saved. My student pulled her car to the side of the road, ran back, and got the kitten. Then, having no idea where it had come from, she gave it to her cousins who had just lost a kitten. Cousins and kitten were last reported doing well.

That kitten did better than others who wander onto the highway.

While we were camping at Waimanalo Beach Park, there was this screeching of car tires and a big thump. My friends and I ran to the road and there was this big puppy lying on the road. He was still moving his head and whimpering. Cars kept coming, barely missing him. Nobody wanted to pick up the puppy, not my friends or the other campers. I guess they were afraid that they would get bitten or get run over by a passing car. Maybe they could have been afraid of what other people might think. I hesitated at first because of those reasons, but I couldn't let the puppy get run over by another car. So I took off my jacket and wrapped my hands and went to pick up the injured puppy. I got him to the side of the road. There was no bleeding, but he still couldn't walk. I took him to the camp site and after a while he started to walk, but there was a slight limp. The next morning he disappeared.

Less fortunate are those dogs and cats who cash in altogether on the road. Even in death, however, they present a traffic problem, with cars swerving around them. Several students report stopping to drag dead animals off the highway. Some have called the Humane Society afterward, others have taken the time to bury the bodies.

Some traffic obstructions are more of an annoyance than a danger. How many times have you found yourself trapped in traffic that is unaccountably inching forward? Eventually, you can see up ahead that your lane is merging into another, and that's causing the slowdown. Finally, you reach the problem itself: a trash can lying in the middle of the lane, or a traffic cone that's been knocked out of place, or a branch or board, or any of the other obstacles my students report. What do you do in such a situation? If you are like most people, you wait your turn in line and then, when you get a chance, you drive around the obstacle and continue on your way.

I noticed this social problem when I was on my way to pick my husband up from work. There was a large piece of wood lying in the middle of the right-hand lane, blocking that lane. As I automatically crossed over to the left-hand side of the road to avoid it, I thought to myself that someone should move it. A little farther down the road it hit me that I was just as capable, if not more so since I had the chance to earn five points in sociology, as anyone else of moving it.

On my way back home, I noticed that the wood was still blocking the right-hand lane, so I stopped my car and picked it up.

Other students have stopped their cars and thrown trash cans off the roads. They've replaced loose manhole covers, moved beer bottles, traffic cones, coconut trees, and so forth.

How about this situation? Have you ever been here? You are sitting in inchworm traffic, see your lane merging to the left, and eventually you realize there's a stalled car in your lane causing the tie-up. What do you do? Usually, you wait your turn, pull around the stalled car, and continue on your way. Several students report stopping to push the stalled car to the side of the road. Not a big project, but it's big enough to restore the flow of traffic. The same can be said for those students who took the time to fix traffic signs that had been bent to point in the wrong directions, those who replanted signs that had been knocked down, and even those who called the traffic department to get action, got none, and called again and again until the job was done. With all the dragons slain and gone, that's the stuff that modern heroism is about.

A couple of us were standing at the corner of Kapiolani and Keeamoku waiting for the crosswalk signal. I noticed the lane nearest to us was coned, and a cone closest to the intersection had been knocked down into the lane. This caused cars to swerve into the oncoming traffic to avoid hitting it. When the "WALK" signal finally flashed, and with my heart pounding in my ears, I dashed straight for the cone, uprighted it, avoided looking at anyone and walked across as if nothing had happened.

It was outright scary, but the personal satisfaction I felt was so different from anything I'd ever done before. I realized I had the guts to do something that I'd ordinarily leave for someone else to do. And, by the way, I'll try it again even without five points backing me up.

Buses and Bus Stops

A common problem for bus riders is messy seats. You've probably gotten on a crowded bus and moved toward the unaccountably empty seat—only to find a puddle of water or a melted candy bar on it. Usually passengers simply put up with such inconveniences, waiting for the bus company to clean the seats—which must be at least every two weeks. Several of my students have taken it upon themselves to wipe up the mess and make the seat usable. Although they generally try to do it inconspicuously, they tend to report people staring at them, and feeling embarrassed about their "good deed."

How many times have you gotten on a bus and noticed that someone had left something behind? Maybe you've had an experience like that of this student, who noticed a purse lying on the seat across from her.

I thought "I'll let someone else get up and return it to the bus driver. It's not my responsibility, and besides, I don't want to make a fool of myself."

So I sat back and watched the people get on, hoping someone would turn the purse in to the driver. To my surprise, everyone just passed by the seat, looked at the purse, and then sat somewhere else! I thought, "Wow! What happened to everyone's sense of honesty and responsibility? What a shame!" Then it occurred to me that I myself was just as guilty as the next person for not returning the purse.

With that realization, she got up, took the purse to the driver, and returned to her seat. "As I sat down, I didn't care what the other passengers were thinking nor whether or not I made a fool of myself. I just felt proud of myself for doing someone a favor."

One student had a bus problem that dragged out through the whole semester we were together. In fact, he told me that the problem had been around for three years before that. Living in a remote, rural area, his mother was dependent on the bus for getting to work. Unfortunately, the bus often passed by early, and she would arrive at the bus stop to find herself stranded. My student asked if that constituted a social problem for the optional project. I said he could get extra credit, but only if he actually solved the problem.

A week later, my student reported that he had talked to the bus driver. "Was the problem solved?" I asked. The student admitted that the bus was still early sometimes. No credit.

Two weeks later, he proudly showed me the petition he had circulated among the bus passengers, demanding that the bus keep to its schedule and not pass by stops early. Nevertheless, the bus still came early at times. No credit.

Step by step, the student persisted. By the end of the semester, he had met with the county director of mass transportation and presented the petition. The director later discussed the matter with the president of the bus company, who called my student to report that he had discussed the matter with the drivers and ordered them to stick to their schedules. By the end of the semester, my student could report that the bus had not been early for a month and a half. Five points.

Bus stops can be as problematic as the buses themselves. I've never figured out who decides which stops get benches, but I've been aware all along who keeps them functioning—*nobody*. Thus, one student noticed the concrete bench at his stop was covered with muddy footprints. Nobody could use it. Finally he got a bucket of water and scrubbed it clean.

It was pretty embarrassing, but what amazed me was that some people stared at me as if I were doing something wrong when really what I was doing was for the benefit of everyone else who goes to the bus stop.

This girl had a pleasanter experience handling a broken wooden bench.

Unfortunately, I am not a skilled carpenter. However, with the supervision of my father (who is quite handy) we used a few nails and it was as good as new. Also, there was a board missing, so my father measured the others and we replaced the missing one.

Sometimes getting others to assist you becomes a bit problematic. One student found her social problem in the form of a large metal trash can sitting at a bus stop. The collection of candy wrapper and soda bottles inside had created a large colony of bees, posing a threat to everyone waiting at the bus stop.

Since the trash can was too heavy for my student, she went to a nearby filling station and asked an attendant to give her a hand. She reports that he reluctantly agreed. His reluctance increased when she suggested that they spray the can with insecticide—asking if he had any at the station. His reluctance gave way to panic when he sprayed insecticide into the trash can and was greeted by a massive swarm of bees.

The man himself had not been too excited about helping out in the first place, and as he searched for the bug spray, I felt a real resentment coming from him. At that point, I wished I could have turned and run away. I felt a bit foolish. As we sprayed the bees and they began flying around us, we dodged and swatted at the bees. I laughed a little bit and that seemed to release a little of the tension. But after we had moved the trash can, I thanked him for helping me and he just said "Yah" and walked back to his desk. I was glad when my bus came and I could leave that scene.

Public Toilets

Buses and bus stops may get messy, but they can't compare with public toilets when it comes to opportunities to make a difference in the world. Undoubtedly, our embarrassment over body wastes makes it worse. It's bad enough to have people see you clean up a messy bus seat, but imagine how it would feel to do the same in a public toilet. Several of my students no longer have to *imagine* what it would be like.

Several students have found themselves waiting in line for a toilet, only to discover everyone avoiding one of the stalls. Usually, the problem is that the toilet is unflushed and looks generally disgusting. The problem can often be solved by someone simply flushing the offending toilet. But what an embarrassing thing to do! It's no wonder that people stand in line rather than face that embarrassment. You have to admire someone who's willing to overcome that embarrassment. But how many people do you know who will go to these lengths?

> I went to Kahala Mall to do my Christmas shopping. After a few hours of shopping, I wanted to use the restroom. When I located the restroom, several ladies were waiting in line for their turn. Only two of the three toilets were occupied. I took a look at the third toilet. It was plugged up with toilet paper and sanitary napkins. The water was up to the rim of the bowl. The floor was wet and slippery.
>
> I borrowed a plunger from maintenance and used it to drain the toilet, after removing the sanitary napkin and some toilet paper clumped together with a hollow pipe which I found conveniently placed in the restroom.
>
> When I used the plunger to fix the toilet and cleaned the floor with paper towels, I could sense the "eyes" the ladies were giving me. When I finished cleaning, I looked at the ladies and they gave me the weirdest look. I did get the feeling that they thought that I was the culprit for the mess, so I was cleaning it.

If you found yourself getting a little queasy reading that report (I did), then you know exactly the feeling that keeps us from ever doing anything about problems like that. It's the same when someone gets sick and throws up in a public bathroom. One student said that happened in his dormitory, so he decided to clean it up.

Those who didn't know I didn't do it laughed politely when they saw me, some snickered quietly. One guy said "Ugh. Gross!" Some who knew I didn't do it said, "How come you gotta clean 'em up?" or just laughed nervously. One guy said, "Alright!" Some people just came in, did their business and rushed out.

Why *did* he clean it up if he didn't make the mess? Was it the five points? That probably helped, but I especially liked the student's concluding comment: "It wasn't as hard to clean as it looked, and it was easier to clean than to spend a day smelling and seeing that stuff."

Dormitory bathrooms have other problems. Two have been reported as often as anything else. Wet counters are an annoyance; you can get your shirt wet just looking in the mirror. Several students report buying sponges and leaving them on the counter—and they report good results. Water on the floor, usually from flooded showers, is more than an annoyance; it's a hazard. Several students have unclogged drains, others have gotten janitors to do it. One student spread his newspaper on the floor to soak up the water. The janitor cleaned up the paper but didn't fix the drain. The next day, my student spread his paper out again. This continued several days until the janitor finally agreed to fix the shower. General cleaning, however, is the staple in this genre. In case you'd like to experiment with this one, here's a checklist for you to follow:

I cleaned the floors of rubbish, made sure the trash cans were neat and in place, replaced toilet paper rolls, made the stalls neat and even flushed the unflushed toilets. I also dusted the tile shelf. This was a first-time experience for me and of course I felt conspicuous. Because of the people,

I felt embarrassed but did my best to ignore the wierd faces and stares. Some girls whispered to their friends, shrugged their shoulders, and went off laughing. That was a little discouraging. But then there was one lady who was concerned and asked me why I'm doing all this when the janitors have that duty. After I explained, she praised the project and wished me good luck. I made that rest room look ten times better and I'm proud of myself. In spite of what I had to go through, it feels good inside.

Living Together

Dormitory life has problems even when the toilets are working. If you've ever lived in group quarters, you'll find some of these problems familiar. Communal kitchens aren't cleaned, lounge furniture gets messed up, and there's noise, noise, noise.

We have to put up with lawn mowers outside as early as seven o'clock in the morning and trucks that have bells that ring when they back up as early as six-thirty. At night, people are yelling and music is blasting as late as midnight.

Conversations with the dormitory staff, the head resident, and the student housing office handled most of this student's problems. The lawn mowing was rescheduled, quiet hours were enforced, and the truck bells . . . well, he learned to love the bells. He concludes, "The major part of the noise problem is now solved and my dormitory is now quiet and all two hundred of us have benefitted from my actions."

There is no end to the variety of noises hassling dormitory residents. I loved this report and the way the student described handling it.

The social problem that I was faced with involved the dreadful sound of the bathroom door in our dorm. The cause was that one of the sheets of plywood that comprises the two sides of the door was slowly breaking loose at the top corner of our door. Thus, whenever the door was opened or closed, it got caught on the door frame, making an irritating noise.

To solve this problem, I first got a thumbtack to pin the piece of wood down, but that didn't seem to solve the problem. So instead, I asked around, found a nail, and hammered it in with my door stopper.

Another student was troubled by "a squeaky trash chute door that wakes us up and disturbs our sleep." This student got some oil and oiled the hinges on the chute door. Then he did something quite common in the reports students give.

I figured if this was a problem to our one floor, the other apartment residents on the other floors must have experienced the same problem. I went to the other twelve floors and did the same for each of the trash chute doors.

Although I suggest that my students fix things because *they* want them fixed, not as a righteous "good deed," the real satisfaction is usually reported in terms of the impact the project has for others. Having things the way you want them is a fair and just payoff for your efforts, and seeing the value you've provided others is a powerful bonus. Thus the student who was bothered by a door that wouldn't stay open searched around to find a doorstop for it. Just as she put it in place, another dorm resident came by with her arms full and obviously appreciated my student's project. She concludes, however, "I noticed several other doors that had previously always been closed were now kept open with a doorstop."

Another student faced the difficulty of taking and getting messages via communal telephones. Finally, she "decided to buy message pads for each telephone on my floor and also pens to go with the message pads." Cautiously, she also left a note with each, asking the girls to *leave* the pads and pens by the phones. She reports the project worked fine. People are getting their messages now, and she concludes, "I see my pink message slips on a lot of doors."

Very often, dorm residents face the problem of all wanting to do something but each being afraid to be the first. Once one person steps forward, the rest follow. This student shared a bathroom with ten or twelve others, and she reports that each of them trucked their "towels, shampoo, conditioners, toothbrushes, toothpastes, soap, etc.) back and forth to the bathroom every time they used it.

> It's a problem when you're all wet and have to lug all this stuff back to your room and when you drop things and bend over to pick them up and your towel falls off right when a guy just happens to be walking down the hall.

Is that what's bothering you? The solution was obvious to my student. The girls should all leave their stuff in the bathroom, with the consequent danger of theft. My student took the lead and left her stuff in the bathroom, convincing her roommate to do the same. After a couple of days, a few others had done the same, but the idea didn't really catch on. So she started talking to the other girls on a one-to-one basis, inviting them to just trust each other.

> The first time I did it, a girl who saw me asked me if I wasn't afraid someone might come and steal my expensive shampoo and conditioner. I just replied that I thought everyone I met on the floor so far seemed really nice and honest and if someone actually did grab my stuff, they probably needed it more than I did.

She reports that the project is now working well. She, too, concludes by commenting on the impact it had on others. "They had made a decision to trust and it felt good. It also gave them a good feeling to be trusted and I seriously doubt that anyone will get ripped off."

The Opportunities Are Everywhere for Everyone

It should be clear by now that my students have had no trouble finding opportunities for heroism in the modern world. But don't let yourself slip into thinking this is just something for college students taking a sociology course. Over the years, most of the people I have described the project to have later reported to me about situations they found themselves in— where they were able to try out a little social responsibility to see how it worked.

From time to time, I receive letters from students who didn't do the project during the class—but did so subsequently. For example, one of my summer school students, Maureen, later wrote to say, "Last September when I returned to teaching in St. Louis, my 'somebody should do something about that' situation hit me in the face." The problem was parking. "You should have heard the grumbles every morning as people entered the building complaining about searching for a space in which to park!" Maureen decided to take on the problem.

She went first to the principal, who described all his past ineffective efforts to solve the problem. Next she discussed the situation with the union representative in the building, receiving more explanations of why nothing could be done about the problem. Undeterred, Maureen wrote to the president of the union's local chapter. Her letter was forwarded to the superintendent of public schools, who ordered an investigation of the situation. As soon as the weather permitted, a portion of a huge school yard was paved, and the teachers were soon parking in a fenced parking lot. Maureen summarized her feelings. "It's nice to know as a 'little person' I do count."

9. BARRIERS TO TAKING RESPONSIBILITY

The heroes, the saints and sages—they are those who face the world alone.
    —*Norman Douglas*

It should be evident by now that the opportunities for modern heroism are virtually infinite. Every day presents us with a continually unfolding menu of chances for greatness. I'm not talking here of just doing "nice" things, but of opportunities to make a difference—big and small—in the quality of life around us. Often such opportunities require little or no effort and no risk of injury or death. Yet, for the most part, we don't take those opportunities.

We have already had glimpses of the reasons for passing up those opportunities for greatness. In this chapter, I want to face them all head-on. As we'll see, there *are* risks. For the most part, those risks are not physical: they are social. At the bottom line, today's heroes risk being thought of badly by those around them. Let's see some of the variations on that theme.

I'll Seem "Goody-Goody"

A theme common in the reports from students that I discussed in chapter 8 was the fear of having their good works seen as "goody-goody." Several students reported that they stopped to pick up trash while walking down the street with friends. The reaction was virtually identical in all cases: "What are you, some kind of good-goody?" Then the hard part began. Picking up trash was easy. Explaining why was something else.

Early on in the course, I gave students permission to alibi by saying something like: "I have this nutty professor who'll give me course credit for doing this. I'm not really all that nice." They always laughed when I told them that, and most reported they had had to use the alibi out there in the trenches of doing good.

The simple fact is that we demean people who do those things we actually think we should have done. When *you* bend down to pick up a candy wrapper, the little voice in the back of *my* head starts sounding like my mother or my old scoutmaster. "Why didn't *you* pick up that candy wrapper, Earl?" I have the feeling someone behind me is shaking their finger at me disapprovingly. To justify my failure to "do right," I make you wrong. The simplest solution is to ridicule you as some namby-pamby who never grew up and learned how things are in the real world. I decide you've probably never heard of hardball. You're probably still hooked on Bambi and Thumper. What a goody-goody! I'm sure glad I'm not like that.

That's the sort of thing you can look forward to if you take responsibility for public problems, and that's one of the good reasons why you and I pass up the opportunities for heroism so often.

I'll Seem "Holier Than Thou"

A variation on the "goody-goody" theme is "holier than thou." Obviously if your good works make me feel that you *are* more righteous than me, I'm certainly going to assume that's a part of your motivation. Maybe it is.

Certainly doing good has gotten a bad name, largely out of the self-righteousness of the "do-gooders." I'm sure you can recall experiences with such people, and you probably don't enjoy it anymore than anyone else. But here's the problem. You and I have associated doing good so closely with self-righteousness that we have trouble separating one from the other. And we're not alone in that.

If you take on some social problem, committing yourself to the common good, you are likely to be held aside as uncomfortably different from "regular" folks. You may learn how ministers, priests, and rabbis often feel.

A funny thing happened on the way to civilization that has made it virtually impossible to do "nice" things without feeling embarrassed, without having to apologize or explain. Consider this situation.

Imagine you're seated on a fairly crowded bus. All the seats are taken, and there are two or three people standing in the aisle. The bus stops, and an elderly woman gets on board, carrying a large shopping bag. There's no seat available for her, and all the seated passengers—you included—suddenly begin studying their fingernails or picking lint off their clothes. As the bus starts up and rocks its way down the street, the woman staggers from one side of the aisle to the other, stumbles into another standing passenger, apologizes, and then is smashed into the seat in front of you. She drops her shopping bag, and stuff spills out. As the bus continues swerving back and forth, the woman bounces from one side of the aisle to the other. Every time she hits your side, she picks up something more from the spilled shopping bag.

Finally, you get up and offer her your seat. Now you are standing up, with all the other passengers looking at you. What is it that you want to tell them? What do you try to communicate through your facial expressions and gestures?

> Look, I'm not really that nice. I'm no goody-goody. I'm as cool and suave as you. I was just afraid that clumsy old woman was going to step on my new shoes. I didn't really give up my seat anyway; I just got up so I could leave the bus at my stop.

To prove your point, you get off the bus ten blocks from your house and walk the rest of the way home in the rain. Better to get soaked and ruin your new shoes than to have all those people staring at you, thinking you were some kind of self-righteous goody-goody.

The Demise of Virtue

Ironically, "virtue" has gotten a bad name. I know it's not cool or sophisticated to discuss virtue these days. To do so is to seem old-fashioned, humorless, and conservative. But to understand why you and I so often pass up the opportunity for heroism, it is important to look virtue straight in the eye.

If you have any doubts about the unacceptability of virtue today, try this experiment. The next time you are in a group of people—it doesn't really matter if they are friends or strangers—make this announcement: "I just wanted to remind everyone to be Trustworthy, Loyal, Helpful, Friendly, Courteous, Kind, Obedient, Cheerful, Thrifty, Brave, Clean, and Reverent." See how people react to that.

Whenever I've read that list to my college classes (sociologists can do anything), I've noticed that my students fidget a lot, study their fingernails, and pick lint off their clothes. There's something uncomfortable about confronting such a heavy dose of virtue all at once, and I want to look at why that's so.

To begin, I think we could agree that virtually all the individual characteristics making up the Scout Law are, on the whole, desirable ones. Given the choice between entering into a business deal with someone who is trustworthy versus someone who is untrustworthy, for example, I suspect we'd both choose the former over the latter. Given the choice between friends who defend us versus those who cut us down behind our backs, I'd guess that loyalty would pretty consistently win over disloyalty.

Lost in a strange city, I think both you and I would prefer to have someone show us how to get where we wanted to go instead of making an obscene gesture or pointing us toward the shortcut through Muggers' Lane. Friendly, courteous, and kind people are surely more enjoyable to be around than are hostile, rude, and cruel ones. By the same token, all of us would prefer sitting down on an airplane beside someone basically cheerful rather than someone intent on filling our airborne hours with stories of how badly life had been treating him or her.

The notion of "obedience" is a little more problematic because of the authoritarian-submissive connotations it sometimes carries. Still, we'd probably agree that young children do well to obey their parents, and employees have some obligation to do what their supervisors tell them to do.

By the same token, we might not honor the image of the miserly skinflint, but in general, responsible financial management is to be preferred over mismanagement and bankrupcy.

I know that both you and I would rather walk down Muggers' Lane with someone brave than with a coward. And while we might disagree on how close cleanliness is to godliness, we would probably choose—all else equal—cleanliness over filth.

And finally, we might have a discussion over the importance of reverence as long as that was attached to specific religious rituals, but I doubt that we'd have any trouble agreeing on the desirability of a having a decent respect for our value and dignity as human beings.

In short, with the possibility of some minor quibbling here and there, we could probably agree that the Boy Scout Law goes a long way toward describing the qualities we'd value in associates. At the very least, we could agree that each item is preferable to its opposite.

But suppose you're at a party. You've gotten all dressed up, and you look really good. Moreover, you've worked hard at being an intelligent conversationalist, discussing all the right topics knowledgeably and expressing all the right opinions with conviction. You know you're doing great. Then, your host says "Oh, here's someone I want you to meet." You look up and there is *the one*. Bells ring, fireworks explode, a symphony orchestra begins. This could be the person you've been waiting for all your life. I mean, this is Prince Charming or the Fairy Princess. Then your host begins touting your virtues: trustworthy, loyal, helpful, friendly. . . . You slowly die a thousand deaths. It's worse than finding you've got broccoli in your teeth. As soon as you can escape your host, the first thing you'll clarify is that you are not really like that.

The reason we don't want people to think we're so virtuous is because of how *we* despise virtuous people. Their virtues seem to highlight all our own failures and shortcomings. While I regard myself as fundamentally trustworthy, for example, if I became convinced that you were *absolutely* trustworthy, you would be a constant reminder to me of all those times I proved to be untrustworthy. Meeting you and being around you would lead me to recall all those times I had broken my word, gone back on a promise, or failed to meet an obligation. All that would bring up the uncomfortable fear that perhaps I'm not really as trustworthy as I think I am. There are two possible solutions to this problem.

First, I can put you down for being "too" trustworthy. That is to say, you are too zealous about this trustworthy business, too uptight. I suspect you probably don't have a sense of humor. Given your rigid commitment to absolutes, you probably have authoritarian tendencies, a closet fascist. I'll bet your children don't really love you.

The second alternative is to discover you're not as virtuous as you pretend. This is better, actually. Nothing sells newspapers faster than the exposure of self-righteous hypocrites. It's always a comfort to know that a wealthy person cheated to get ahead. If it had been only a matter of hard work, you and I might feel lazy by comparison. When someone rich and famous gets divorced, we can comfort ourselves in the righteousness of having put our families ahead of success.

John Kennedy and his presidential Camelot made a lot of people like us feel pretty lowly until we heard that he had been cheating on Jackie. What a relief! Jimmy Carter was an even greater threat until he confessed to lusting in his heart. That was better than nothing.

Blaine Harden suggests this pattern has been around for a while.

> Civilizations throughout history have taken perverse delight in turning on heroes, holding them up to impossible standards, digging up dirt about their private lives and concluding, after all, that the hero is flawed and self-seeking—certainly no better than us.[1]

The Hawaiians speak of a "crab-pot mentality" in this regard. When Hawaiian fishermen go crabbing, they simply throw the crabs they catch into a bucket. While you might wonder why the crabs don't crawl out of the bucket, the Hawaiians learned long ago that there was no danger of that. Whenever one crab reaches the lip of the bucket and starts to crawl out, the other crabs grab it—seeking their own escape—and, ultimately, pull the leader back into the pot. While Hawaiians often criticize themselves for having this "crab-pot mentality," it seems to be pretty fundamentally human.

If you act on your opportunity for heroism, therefore, if you choose to take personal responsibility for public affairs, about the best you can expect is that you'll be despised for your apparent virtue. More likely, however, others will deny your virtue altogether.

When Samantha Smith, the eleven-year-old from Maine, began getting media coverage for her correspondence with Yuri Andropov, Nicholas Daniloff labeled her a "Pawn in Propaganda War," in the conservative *U.S. News & World Report.* In the liberal *New Republic,* on the other hand, Charles Krauthammer would write, "I concede that Samantha is not a Communist dupe. My question is: Who cares?"

My Motives Will Be Suspect

A few years ago, when I first read something about the Guardian Angels, my immediate thought was: "What a great idea." I was really pleased that someone was doing what Curtis Sliwa's people were doing. Shortly thereafter, I began reading negative reports about the Angels. In particular, the press began suggesting that the Angels were only in it for the personal glory. Sliwa was on an ego trip. The proof of this lay in the high public visibility of the Angels, and Sliwa was characterized as a "publicity-seeker."

The later, negative reports were depressing to me. Like many others, I suspect, I was disappointed that the Angels weren't what they first seemed to be. I suppose I was mildly annoyed that I had been taken in again by a slick con man. I'm sure I wasn't alone in those feelings.

Sometime later, however, the absolute absurdity of the "publicity-seeking" charge hit me. As we saw in chapter 4, the purpose of the Guardian Angels is to create a "visual deterrent" to street crime. Their intention is to make it known that they will intervene in rapes, muggings, and other street violence if they see it happening. Their presence on the street—dramatized by their red berets and white T-shirts—is a signal that crimes could not be committed with impunity.

When I recalled this fundamental purpose of the Guardian Angels, I immediately recognized the stupidity in the criticism of "publicity-seeking." Of course they would—and *should*—seek publicity. Otherwise, how could they be a visual deterrent?

If you recall the movie *Dr. Strangelove,* you may recall the ultimate, bizarre joke in the film. The Russians had created a Doomsday Machine that would destroy the world if Russia were attacked. This has been a semiserious fantasy for years among those who seek to achieve peace through bigger bombs. The bizarre joke was that the Russians in the film *kept the Doomsday Machine secret.* Having created the ultimate deterrent, they didn't tell anyone.

Obviously, the alternative to "publicity-seeking" for the Guardian Angels would be to hide in the shadows and hope for trouble. Then they could spring into action and create the cycle of violence and violent counter-violence that others have sometimes feared the Angels represented.

Virtually every publicized act of heroism will be regarded by some as *only* publicity-seeking. There are two reasons for this. First, you and I have lived through enough genuine publicity-seeking to be wary of anything that may fit the pattern. Second, as I've pointed out repeatedly, we have trouble believing anyone would simply do good. Automatically, we ask, "What's in it for them?"

Near the head of the list of possibilities—alongside ego tripping and publicity-seeking—is *money*. We have a treasury of clichés to warn us that you can't get something for nothing, everybody is out for number one, and so forth.

Thus, if you act on an opportunity for heroism, it is likely that others will think you have some financial angle. When Werner Erhard first initiated The Hunger Project, it was firmly believed—and proclaimed—in some circles that he had found a way to make money out of the misery of the world's starving people. Years later, with a string of unqualified financial audits and no evidence of wrong-doing, the criticism slowly faded away, but I'm sure the suspicion remained for some. After all, why else would anyone commit himself or herself to helping others?

The current state of American politics is such that it is virtually impossible for a politician to do anything genuinely for the public good without suffering snide rumors about his or her "true" motives—usually seen as seeking higher office. I do not mean to suggest that politicians don't often behave as cynically and dishonestly as we tend to think they do. The point is that you and I would have trouble recognizing a genuine act of heroism if it appeared in the political arena.

When George Washington turned down the opportunity to become king of the United States, saying we should be a republic rather than a monarchy, I am certain there were some who were convinced that George was working a special angle. And when he refused a third term, saying the presidency should circulate, there were some convinced that he had a better offer from the colonial equivalent of Bechtel or Boeing.

The point of all this for our present discussion is that you need to expect that your motives will be questioned and the worst thought of you if you choose an act of genuine heroism. It might be useful, at the same time, for you to be more conscious of your own reactions to the heroism of others.

It's Not My Responsibility

This is perhaps the most convincing reason of all for not taking responsibility for public problems. If you didn't cause the problem, why should you solve it? In fact, somebody else is probably being paid to solve such problems, as we saw in chapter 3. It's simply not fair to expect *you* to solve the problem.

If you take on a public problem, chances are that people around you will assume you caused it. This was dramatically demonstrated in the case of several student projects. One student was walking across campus when he noticed a trash can with trash scattered on the ground around it. He decided this was a good opportunity for his project. While he was picking up the trash and putting it in the can, three strangers walked past; one paused long enough to snap: "Clumsy!" Obviously he must have made the mess, or why else would he be picking it up?

If you take on a public problem and can convince people you didn't cause the problem, you are likely to be thought a fool for cleaning up someone else's mess. If the whole thing was your own idea, you are simply weird. If you got the idea from someone else (from this book, for example), you will be seen as having been duped or conned. You can expect to find yourself described as naïve and unsophisticated for not seeing how you have been taken in.

The fact that a particular public problem is not your responsibility—that is, you didn't cause the problem—is a powerful reason for doing nothing. You will need to rise above that reason if you are to be a modern hero. Each of the heroes we've considered in this book has had to do that, however. Neither Rosa Parks nor Martin Luther King, Jr., started segregation in the South. Curtis Sliwa didn't cause street crime in New York, any more than Beowulf caused Grendel to terrorize the castle. Heroism requires *taking* responsibility for a problem you didn't cause.

I Don't Know What to Do

As we saw in chapter 3, life has gotten pretty complicated in many of its aspects. Thus, there are surely many problems facing the nation and the world that you are not equipped to solve. I would guess, for example, that you don't know how to make nuclear power plants truly safe (aside from shutting them down). Few of us have special expertise in the realm of cleaning up chemical and nuclear wastes. "Not knowing what to do," then, is an excellent reason for doing nothing. Like the other barriers to public responsibility, however, it is simply a sellout of your opportunity for heroism.

When you recognize a public problem and don't know how to solve it, you can always demand that those "officially" responsible do something. Consider the example of Judy Piatt, a Missouri horse-breeder. After watching dozens of her horses die in agony, she became convinced that the oil sprayed on her stable floor to keep the dust down was involved.

Piatt began following the trucks that delivered the salvage oil and discovered a number of dangerous chemical dump sites. She sent a list of the sites to state and federal officials. Nothing happened.

She persisted in her demands that action be taken, and after a decade of her insistence, the federal government finally looked into the matter. What they discovered has horrifying. The oil used to spray the roads and private stables was routinely mixed with a sludge rich in dioxin, one of the most toxic compounds on earth. Suddenly a national alert was sounded to uncover and remedy dioxin sites throughout the South and elsewhere in the country. There is no way to guess how many people are alive today who would have died from dioxin poisoning if Judy Piatt had let her lack of technical know-how stop her from taking responsibility for what she perceived as a public problem.

At the very least, you can always make other people aware of the problem you recognize. Even if you can't offer an easy solution, you can draw attention to the problem and the need for a solution.

I May Make Things Worse

The only thing worse than not knowing what to do is thinking you do when you don't. There is no end of stories about well-meaning people who try to do good and inadvertently make matters worse. Seeing smoke rising from the back of your neighbor's house, you start spraying with your garden hose and wipe out a barbeque party. All of us have made mistakes—some big, some small—where our good intentions have gone awry, and such mistakes often make us wary in the future.

Those scholars who study the operation of systems have added to this fear through their research and through some of their concepts. Thus, for example, the notion of "unintended consequences" points directly to the heart of this problem. We take an action with a particular purpose in mind, and, whether the action serves the intended purpose or not, it can have other consequences we never imagined. There are numerous examples from the field of national development.

Suppose you came across a developing country that lacked effective sanitation systems, such that wastes were seeping into the drinking water, causing death, and keeping death rates high. The obviously appropriate action would be to improve the sanitation systems. If you were to do this, as has been done in numerous nations around the world, water pollution would be reduced (good), disease rates would decline (good), as would death rates (good), except that population would then increase (bad), outstripping food supplies (bad), and resulting in mass hunger and starvation (bad). This scenario has been repeated in country after country.

To continue, let's take the example of a rural village in a developing country where the local agriculture is simply insufficient to support the population. Let's say that local farming methods are inefficient and need upgrading. Children are going hungry and dying. The obvious solution, from the standpoint of a rich and generous neighboring nation, would be to provide emergency gifts of food to the village. This action would be taken as a temporary measure, until the local farmers could begin producing enough food for the local population. Unfortunately, the gift of free food means that no one in the village will be interested in buying food from the local growers, thereby destroying an already troubled industry.

In view of such situations, Professor Jay Forrester and his "system dynamics" colleagues at MIT and elsewhere have coined the term, "counter-intuitive reasoning." Since solutions to problems that seem intuitively appropriate so often cause more problems than they solve, Forrester and his colleagues argue that we must be willing to question what seems intuitively correct and be able to move beyond it. For the system dynamicists, computer simulation is the likely method for accomplishing this. By creating computer models that behave like real-life processes, it is possible to make changes to the computer model and see what happens in the long run, prior to taking real-life actions that may be irreversible.

I say all of this to dramatize the power of "I might make things worse" as a reason for doing nothing, as an excuse for turning away from responsibility for social problems. Now, I'd like to counter that reason with two comments.

First, concepts such as "unintended consequences" and "counter-intuitive reasoning" are intended to empower more effective action, not to make us comatose. Our history of past mistakes should make us more effective. Every mistake should add to our knowledge of what doesn't work, so we don't have to make the same mistake again.

Second, picking up litter, calling the street department to report a broken street sign, demanding that your senator do something about nuclear wastes—none of these actions is likely to destroy the ecological balance of nature.

I May Look Stupid

Not knowing what to do and the fear of making things worse both have a common base that actually extends to most of the barriers to taking responsibility for public problems. This is perhaps the foremost obstacle to heroism: "I may look stupid."

In my observations of myself and other people, none of us is terribly threatened by being stupid or doing stupid things—but we are terrified that others will think us stupid. I have done thousands of stupid things that no one knows about (and I'll never tell). For the most part, I've totally forgotten about them. You probably have a similar list of irrelevant past stupidities.

But when you step out of line and take on a public problem, you expose yourself to public view and possible public ridicule. Suppose, for example, you had learned about the rural village I mentioned earlier—the one whose agriculture couldn't support the local population. You might have been deeply moved by the starving children, moved enough that you would speak out in a public meeting and urge that the United States send emergency food supplies. Someone more experienced than you in such matters might point out the negative impact the gift would have on the local economy. They might even add an observation about the danger that corrupt government officials might siphon the food off into the black market, with the profits going into their own pockets. You could look stupid and naïve, and that's a powerful reason for keeping your mouth shut.

Unfortunately, real heroism is inextricably linked to the possibility of looking stupid. That's true of excellence in general, however. There's an old baseball adage that says you can't steal second without taking your foot off first. There are always risks, and we need to weigh the potential costs and benefits.

Nothing I Do Makes a Difference

If all the barriers I have discussed above are the reasons we don't accept opportunities for heroism when they arise, the box those reasons come in is "Nothing I do makes a difference." In my view, this is the primary tragedy of our time. I suggest that you and I live our entire adult lives within the fundamental view that we do not make a difference. This operates in all aspects of our lives, not just in the domain of personal responsibility for public problems.

Every time you have broken your word, you have telegraphed the view that *you* do not make a difference. So you said you'd come to a dinner party, and then cancel at the last minute because you just don't feel like going. Your cancellation says that your presence at the party doesn't matter. People will get along just fine without you.

Any time you cut a class in school, you sent along a message that your being there wouldn't have mattered. This applies equally to every committee meeting you skipped, every place you didn't show up. The fact that life proceeded without you probably justified your view, but it also drove a secret stake into your heart.

This view of not making a difference, which most of us are too polite to discuss, is compounded to the extent that you believe others *do* make a difference. It parallels exactly the view that others are perhaps more righteous than you, and the consequences are the same. Our crab-pot mentality forces us to drag others down, denying that they make a difference either. Ultimately, we emasculate ourselves as a human race.

I am neither prepared nor inclined to jack you up and convince you that you really do make a difference. Ultimately, making a difference is not a function of evidence, as much as we may seek it. It is a function of personal declaration. You must choose for yourself whether your life will be about making a difference or whether it will be about getting by until you achieve the release of death.

Each of the heroes we have examined in this book has had to make that declaration for himself or herself. Each has had to say, evidence to the contrary perhaps, "I do and will make a difference—because I say so." Every morning for ten lonely years, Sidney Rittenberg awoke with the crushing realization that he was still in prison. Every morning, he rededicated his life to making a contribution to his planet. That is the fundamental opportunity available to you right now, today, this minute. No matter how many times you have passed up the opportunity in the past, that opportunity for heroism persists. I invite you to take it.

10. THE LITTLE INDIVIDUAL

To have a chance to do one's share in shaping the laws of the whole country spreads over one the hush that one used to feel when one was waiting the beginning of a battle. . . . We will not falter. We will not fail. We will reach the earthworks if we live, and if we fail we will leave our spirit in those who follow, and they will not turn back. All is ready. Bugler, blow the charge.

—Oliver Wendell Holmes
(Bidding farewell to his staff
to join the U.S. Supreme
Court)

If there were a prototype for the kind of hero described in this book, it would be R. Buckminster Fuller (1895–1983), and I've dedicated the book to Bucky.[1] As a young man, early in this century, Bucky chose to make his life an experiment. He estimated that the experiment would take about fifty years, and it addressed the question: What can the "little individual" do on behalf of the planet?

Bucky recognized that governments and powerful corporations could have enormous impact on the quality of life on Earth. But what could one individual do? What would be the result of a single individual, occupying no official position, living life from the point of view of the whole planet?

It is altogether fitting to end this book with a brief review of Bucky's eighty-eight years on the planet. As you look at how you will live the remainder of your years on earth, you could have no better model for your life.

Bucky's life-long experiment began in despair. Following service as a naval officer during World War I, he tried his hand at a few diverse jobs and eventually found himself in Chicago with his wife Anne and his young daughter Alexandra, as partner in his father-in-law's building construction firm. While his prospects were at first bright, it was all to change dramatically. Alexandra caught the flu, then was stricken by spinal meningitis. Finally, she was crippled by infantile paralysis. When Alexandra died in 1923, Bucky was crushed, feeling he had been somehow responsible by not providing a better environment for her. He began drinking heavily and tried to bury himself in his work, but to no avail. By 1927, the building company had failed, losing all of Bucky's money and a great deal of money invested by his friends. By his own judgment, he was an utter failure in life.

In the depth of his depression, Bucky went to the shore of Lake Michigan and seriously considered suicide. He had not been able to provide for his helpless daughter. He was a failure in business, broke, and discredited among his friends. He had drawn the remains of his life into a bottle. Bucky Fuller as a human being seemed to represent little of value to his family, his community, or his planet. Ending his life seemed the appropriate thing to do.

Years later, during World War II, American soldiers in the Pacific theater confronted a strange phenomenon. Having faced the fanatical self-sacrifice of Japanese soldiers, they were astounded by those who were somehow captured alive. Unaccountably, they cooperated totally with their captors, answering their questions about Japanese military strength and plans. Anthropologists offered an explanation.

It was considered a Japanese soldier's duty to either be victorious or die in battle. Being captured was, strangely, the same as dying. The Japanese soldiers knew their families would henceforth regard them as dead. Their old lives had now ended, and their continued life was a strange existence, no longer governed by the old norms.

Standing on the shore of Lake Michigan, Bucky Fuller underwent a similar transformation. It was as though he had given up his old life and any conventional claim on it. Rather than throw his body into the lake, however, he chose to use the gift of continued life on behalf of his planet.

In 1927, I resolved to do my own thinking, and see what the individual, starting without any money or credit—in fact, with considerable discredit, but with a whole lot of experience—to see what the individual, with a wife and new-born child [Allegra], could produce on behalf of his fellow men.

Bucky's question was: What could the little individual do that governments, armies, and large corporations could not do? What could an individual achieve if he or she operated from a sense of responsibility for the planet rather than from the individual needs and desires that more typically govern our lives?

This was to be a fifty-year experiment to prove that man, like nature, was not a failure but a success; to rethink everything I knew. It was an experiment in which I myself was the guinea pig. I had to begin from the beginning. I had to find out what man has and see how it can be used for the advantage of others. I became convinced that we're here for each other.

Looking for ways in which the world could be made to work for everyone, Bucky contrasted his experience in the navy with that in the building construction industry. A fundamental principle at sea was to "do more with less," a principle that was to inform most of his remaining life's work. In contrast to ship design, land-based buildings gained their strength from sheer mass of steel and concrete. Bucky set out to change all that.

The Dymaxion House was a true revolution in building design. Housing a family of five, it was a "house on a pole." The hexagonal structure was suspended by cables from a missile-like mast rising through its center. Both inside and out, the

Dymaxion House is still futuristic more than half a century later. Air was drawn in through the central mast, after which it was filtered and washed, cooled or heated, rendering the dwelling virtually dust-free. Water was filtered, sterilized, and recycled, so there was little need for piped-in water. Everything was built-in and many of the cabinets were controlled by intricate light beams.

All its futuristic gadgets notwithstanding, the Dymaxion House was true to Bucky's guiding principle of doing more with less. Whereas a conventional single-family house at that time weighed approximately 150 tons, Bucky's creation was a mere 3 tons. It could be mass-produced, and Bucky anticipated having units air-lifted by zeppelin to remote areas such as the North Pole.

Since his intention was to find a way of serving the interests of humankind rather than his own self-interest, Bucky offered in 1928 to transfer all rights to the Dymaxion House to the American Institute of Architects. His offer was refused, with an explanation that the organization was opposed to mass-produced houses.

At about this time, Bucky had an opportunity to test his commitment to his proclaimed experiment and to learn a lesson about making a difference in the world. In line with his fundamental rejection of the conventional norms of living, Bucky had taken to wearing T-shirts, sneakers, and casual clothes at a time when "respectable" people were expected to dress more formally. The rejection of his Dymaxion House somewhat hardened his rebellion against social conventions. Invited to a formal dinner, he was likely to show up in old clothes and, by his own description, be obnoxiously self-righteous about his views of things.

Eventually, he recognized that his behavior was interfering with his purpose in life.

I was putting self and comfort ahead of my Dymaxion House, and I said, "You're not allowed to do that. You must get over that. You must stop that looking eccentric, with everybody pointing at this guy."

With this realization, Bucky set out to "become the invisible man," taking the bank clerk as his model. He began wearing a black suit so "they would focus on what I was saying instead of my eccentricities."

Bucky's Dymaxion House never has become very popular, but another of his building construction ideas was to make him world famous. Bucky began by recognizing that although the square or rectangle was implicitly taken to be the fundamental element in most building projects, the triangle was far more stable and stronger. And triangles could be fit together to form hexagons, or pentagons which, in turn, could be packed together like the cells of a honeycomb. Thus arrived the geodesic dome, that amazing structure capable of enclosing large areas with no interior supports. Because of its ingenious structural design, the dome weighs little in relation to the job it does, and, as more stress is placed on it, the dome becomes stronger rather than weaker. Like the Dymaxion House, the geodesic dome lends itself to mass production and is easily transported and assembled, resulting in its use by the government at inaccessible locations such as the North Pole. By the time of his death, Bucky estimated there were more than three hundred thousand geodesic domes scattered around the world, covering more acreage than any other type of shelter.

While the geodesic dome was surely Bucky's most famous creation, it was only one of a great many. In addition to his other inventions in connection with the building industry, for example, there was the Dymaxion Car: a streamlined, three-wheeled vehicle with front-wheel drive and rear steering. It was the opposite of just about everything in the conventional cars of the 1930s. Moreover, it was exceptionally stable and maneuverable, and its ninety-horsepower engine could take the car up to 120 miles per hour.

Bucky's Dymaxion Map provides a flat view of the Earth that

has virtually no distortion, unlike the Mercator projection with its overwhelming Greenland and Antarctica. His World Game has offered educational recreation to millions.

Quite aside from his work as an architect, scientist, or engineer, Bucky was widely respected as a philosopher and was appointed Harvard's Charles Eliot Norton Professor of Poetry in 1962. He was often called the planet's "friendly genius," or a modern Leonardo da Vinci. His friend John Denver sang of him as "grandfather of the universe."

For the purposes of this book, Bucky's achievements are less important than their source. You'll recall his life's work was initially designed as an experiment to discover what "the little individual" could accomplish, and he never forgot that.

Increasingly, Bucky would hark back to his early naval experiences and speak of the role of the trim-tab: a tiny movable tab on a ship's rudder. Just as the rudder—small in comparison with the ship's mass—turns the entire ship, so the tiny trim-tab moves the rudder. In Bucky's vision, there was no world problem so great that it could not be impacted by the little individual, acting as a trim-tab.

Paradoxically, you and I cannot survive as solitary individuals in today's world, yet neither can we survive unless we are willing to take personal responsibility, *as individuals,* for the whole. This book has aimed to honor the many heroes who walk among us and to reveal the hero that lives within us all. I'm bothered that the book has unavoidably ignored so many genuine heroes—including close friends whose heroism I've witnessed firsthand and often. We don't honor our heroes enough, and I'd like to see us change that.

In titling this book, *You Can Make a Difference,* I realize that you probably knew that already, and I don't want to invalidate any of the ways you *have* made a difference in the past. At the same time, I know you are probably somewhat embarrassed about your acts of heroism, worried about what people may think. Moreover, if you're anything like me, there have been many times you turned your back on opportunities to make a difference, and some times you've probably tried to deny that you *could* make a difference.

It takes real courage to be human: to commit yourself to greatness, all the while knowing you'll weaken and fall short at times. Only genuine heroes can give it their best shot, fail, give up, and then bounce back.

In all this, you make a difference, not because I say you do, but because you say so. Only *you* can supply the courage to step forward, to take a stand for personal excellence. Yet, whenever one of us is willing to take a chance on heroism, it makes it that much easier for others to do so. This is how we will destroy the deadly conspiracy by which we now keep each other in line.

Inevitably, to talk of making a difference is to evoke feelings of burden, guilt, obligation, and pain. But, let's tell the whole truth.

To make a difference is to look life straight in the eye, to address the whole of life with deep compassion and true power. To make a difference is to experience creation and creativity. It brings an experience of ownership more profound than titles and deeds can ever confer.

Making a difference is the true joy in life, the knowing you've been alive and that your living mattered. I couldn't wish you anything more, nor should you settle for anything less.

Footnotes

1.

1. The Robert Saum episode is taken from Scott Winokur, *San Francisco Examiner and Chronicle,* March 21, 1982, p. A7.

2. The story of Trevor Ferrell is taken from William Plummer and Andrea J. Fine, "Philadelphia's Street People Have Found a Ministering Angel in Tiny Trevor Ferrell," *People,* March 26, 1984, pp. 60–62.

3. The description of PhoneFriend is taken from "Latchkey Children Can Dial a Friend," *The New York Times,* August 14, 1983, p. 21.

4. The Studs Terkel quotations are from Studs Terkel, "Across America There's a Flowing of Life Juices . . ." *Parade,* October 12, 1980, pp. 4–7.

5. The descriptions of ancient Mesopotamian civilization are taken from Samuel Noah Kramer, *Cradle of Civilization* (New York: Time-Life Books, 1967), pp. 11, 13, 40, 64, 70.

6. Isaac Asimov is quoted from "Violence—As Human as Thumbs," *TV Guide,* June 14, 1975, p. 31.

2.

1. The discussion of Farnell's theories about heroism is taken from L. R. Farnell, *Greek Hero Cults and Ideas of Immortality* (Oxford, Eng.: Clarendon Press, 1920).

2. The reference to Joseph Campbell is to his book: *The Hero with a Thousand Faces* (Cleveland: The World Publishing Co., 1968).

3. The story of Audie Murphy is taken primarily from Thomas B. Morgan, "The War Hero," *Esquire,* December 1983, pp. 597–604.

4. The story of Desmond Doss is taken from Boston Herndon, *The Unlikeliest Hero* (Mountain View, Calif.: Pacific Press Publishing Association, 1967).

5. The story of Arland Williams and Lenny Skutnik is taken from Claire Safran, "Hero of the Frozen River," *Reader's Digest,* September 1982, p. 49.

6. The Hart quotation on the different meanings of responsibility are taken from H. L. A. Hart, *Punishment and Responsibility* (New York: Oxford University Press, 1968), p. 211.

7. The story of Shannon Gordon is based on an article by Bonnie Ambler, "A Gift from a Dying Child," *San Francisco Chronicle,* February 13, 1982.

8. The discussion of the Fort Wayne kids is taken from Bob Greene, "When Fort Wayne's Kids Saved the Town," *San Francisco Chronicle,* March 25, 1982.

9. Shawn Ryan's story is taken from "Boy, 7, Saves Mom, Alerts Others to Fire," *San Francisco Chronicle,* February 10, 1984, p. 2.

10. The discussion of Candy Lightner is taken from John J. O'Connor, "TV: 'M.A.D.D.' vs. Drunken Driving," *The New York Times,* March 14, 1983, p. 14; and a letter from Candy Lightner on behalf of MADD.

3.

1. Timothy S. Mescon and Michael H. Mescon are quoted from their article, "More Rigor or Rigor Mortis? It's Your Choice," *SKY*, May 1983, pp. 84–90.

2. Harlan Cleveland's comments are taken from "The Future of Public Administration," *The Bureaucrat*, Fall 1982, pp. 3–8.

3. The story of Lucy Andris is taken from Bob Greene, "Refusing to Let 'the System' Win," *San Francisco Chronicle*, December 31, 1981, p. 11.

4. The story of James McSherry comes from Scott Thompson, "This Truant Officer Really Cares About Attendance," *Christian Science Monitor*, October 27, 1980, p. 20.

5. The discussion of Ernest Fitzgerald is taken primarily from Rebecca Nappi, "Whistle Blower: You Never Recover," *USA Today*, October 11, 1983, p. 8A.

6. Data regarding satisfaction were taken from *Public Opinion*, June/July 1982, and October/November 1982.

7. Data regarding people's attitudes toward government are taken from *Public Opinion*, February/March 1984, p. 29.

8. Voting data reported in this chapter are taken from Bureau of the Census, *Voting and Registration in the Election of November 1982*, Government Printing Office, series P-20, no. 383.

9. Melvin Maddocks is quoted from his article, "It's Not the Best of Times," *Honolulu Advertiser*, January 14, 1979.

10. Data on volunteerism were taken from *Public Opinion*, February/March 1982.

4.

1. The Martin Luther King, Jr., speech in Memphis is quoted from Ira Peck, *The Life and Words of Martin Luther King, Jr.* (New York: Scholastic Book Service, 1974), p. 92.

2. Fear of crime statistics are taken from *Public Opinion,* October/November 1982, p. 36.

3. The story of Stanley Fletcher is taken from Arnold Hamilton, "Like Father, Like Son—Sharing a Prison Cell," *San Francisco Chronicle,* December 16, 1981, p. 72.

5.

1. Portions of this chapter were adapted from Earl Babbie, *Sociology* (3rd ed.) (Belmont, Calif.: Wadsworth, 1983).

2. Philip Boffey is quoted from "Smallpox: Outbreak in Somalia Slows Rapid Progress toward Eradication," *Science,* June 17, 1977, p. 1298–1299. The discussion of smallpox is drawn from Boffey's article, plus Donald Henderson, "The Eradication of Smallpox," *Scientific American,* October 1976, pp. 25–32, and David Zinman, "Good Riddance to Smallpox," *Honolulu Star-Bulletin & Advertiser* October 26, 1976, pp. C-1, C-5.

6.

1. A small portion of this chapter was adapted from Earl Babbie, "Unseating the Horseman: World Hunger," *Honolulu Downtown Magazine,* October 1978, pp. 15–17.

2. Monique Grodzki's story is taken from Cynthia B. Hanson, "Young New Yorkers Take Up the Fight for World Peace," *The Christian Science Monitor,* March 8, 1982, p. 18.

3. The discussion of Harry Chapin was taken from *Food Monitor,* September/October 1981.

7

1. The Nixon–Stevenson exchange is taken from TRB, "The First Step," *New Republic,* Nov 29, 1982, p. 6.

2. The description of Helen Caldicott was taken in part from Robert G. Pushkar, "Helen Caldicott: Anti-Nuclear Crusader," *Parents,* June 1982, pp. 74–76, 130–134.

3. The discussion of Bill Perry is based on a telephone call with him on April 16, 1984.

4. The discussion of Randall Forsberg and the nuclear freeze is taken primarily from "The Nuclear Weapons Freeze Campaign," *The Freeze Focus* (St. Louis, Mo.: Nuclear Weapons Freeze Campaign), March, 1984, p. 2; "Randall Forsberg: A Massachusets Scholar Sounds the Nationwide Call to (Freeze) Arms," *People,* December 27–January 3, 1983, pp. 62–65; and Suzanne Gordon, "The Woman Behind the Freeze," *Mother Jones,* September/October 1982, p. 64.

5. Harold Willens's story is taken from Harold Willens, *The Trimtab Factor* (New York: William Morrow, 1984).

6. The report on Marianne Hamilton and Polly Mann and Women Against Military Madness is based on Kaia Svien, "Peace Tactics: An Action a Day," *MS,* March 1983, p. 21.

7. The discussion of John Marks and The Nuclear Network is taken from Mark Satin, "Nuclear Network Seeks to Transcend Old Peace Movement Rivalries," *Renewal,* May 3, 1982.

8. The report on Gerald Jampolsky and Children as Teachers of Peace is taken from Peggy Taylor, "Children as Teachers of Peace," *NewAge,* November, 1982, and Gerald G. Jampolsky, *Children as Teachers of Peace,* (Tiburon, Calif.: Foundation for Spiritual Alternatives, 1982).

9. Bishop Quinn's story is taken from Mary Ellen Leary, "Nuclear Freeze," *Commonweal,* January 29, 1982, 39–41.

10. Sister Frances Russell's story is taken from "The Nun Who Has Tackled the MX Missile," *San Francisco Chronicle,* December 16, 1983, p. 29.

9.

1. The Blaine Harden quotation is taken from "Filling the Need for Heroes," *Sunday Punch,* February 28, 1982.

10.

1. The discussion of Bucky's life is based largely on *Buckminster Fuller: An Autobiographical Monologue/Scenario,* documented and edited by Robert Snyder (New York: St. Martin's Press, 1980).

10

1. The discussion of Blau's life is based in part on ... ...power ... Robert ... for ... thing. Here is a concise ... developed and edited by Robert Bryce (New York: St. Mar-tin's Press, 1980).